A Bark In The Park -

The 50 Best Places To Hike With Your Dog In The Baltimore Region

Doug Gelbert

illustrations by
Andrew Chesworth

Cruden Bay Books

A BARK IN THE PARK: THE 50 BEST PLACES TO HIKE WITH YOUR DOG IN THE BALTIMORE REGION

Copyright 2002 by Cruden Bay Books

All rights reserved. No part of this book may be reproduced or transmitted in any form or by any means, electronic or mechanical, including photocopying, recording or by any information storage and retrieval system without permission in writing from the Publisher.

Cruden Bay Books
PO Box 467
Montchanin, DE 19710

www.hikewithyourdog.com

International Standard Book Number 0-9644427-7-9

Manufactured in the United States of America

"Dogs are our link to paradise...to sit with a dog on a hillside on a glorious afternoon is to be back in Eden, where doing nothing was not boring - it was peace."
- Milan Kundera

Contents

The 50 Best Places To Hike With Your Dog	29
No Dogs!	133
37 More Places To Hike With Your Dog	135

Also...

Hiking With Your Dog	6
Outfitting Your Dog For A Day Hike	8
Low Impact Hiking With Your Dog	10
The Other End Of The Leash	11
The Best of the Best	
The 10 Best Places To Hike With Your Dog In Greater Baltimore	13
The 10 Best Trails To Hike With Your Dog In Greater Baltimore For Less Than One Hour	18
13 Cool Things To See On Baltimore Trails With Your Dog	22
Dogs At The Atlantic Beaches	154
Dog Parks	156
Index To Parks And Open Space	158

Introduction

The Baltimore region can be a great place to hike with your dog (or "walk" with your dog - for our purposes they are one in the same). Within an hour's drive you can hike on sand trails, climb hills that leave you panting, walk on some of the most historic grounds in America, explore the estates of America's wealthiest families or circle lakes for seven miles and never lose sight of the water.

This book features more than 87 such places within 25 miles of the I-695 Beltway where you can hike with your dog. I have selected, with the help of my 4-year old Border Collie/German Shepherd mix Katie, what I consider to be the 50 best places to take the dog and ranked them according to subjective criteria including the variety of hikes available, opportunities for canine swimming and pleasure of the walks. The rankings include a mix of parks that feature long rambles and parks that contain short walks. In addition, I have also included another 37 places to walk the dog.

For dog owners it is important to realize that not all parks are open to our four-legged friends (see page 133 for a list of parks that do not allow dogs). There are always people agitating for restrictions against dogs and rules pertaining to dogs in our parks can change rapidly - usually for the worst for dog owners. When visiting a park always keep your dog under control and clean up any messes or more and more area parks will be closed to dogs. So grab that leash and hit the trail!

DBG & Katie

Hiking With Your Dog

So you want to start hiking with your dog. Hiking with your dog can be a fascinating way to explore the Baltimore region from a canine perspective. Some things to consider:

🐾 Dog's Health

Hiking can be a wonderful preventative for any number of physical and behavioral disorders. One in every three dogs is overweight and running up trails and leaping through streams is great exercise to help keep pounds off. Hiking can also relieve boredom in a dog's routine and calm dogs prone to destructive habits. And hiking with your dog strengthens the overall owner/dog bond.

🐾 Breed of Dog

All dogs enjoy the new scents and sights of a trail. But some dogs are better suited to hiking than others. If you don't as yet have a hiking companion, select a breed that matches your interests. Do you look forward to an entire afternoon's hiking? You'll need a dog bred to keep up with such a pace, such as a retriever or a spaniel. Is a half-hour enough walking for you? It may not be for an energetic dog like a border collie. If you already have a hiking friend, tailor your plans to his abilities.

🐾 Conditioning

Just like humans, dogs need to be acclimated to the task at hand. An inactive dog cannot be expected to bounce from the easy chair in the den to complete a 3-hour hike. You must also be physically able to restrain your dog if confronted with distractions on the trail (like a scampering squirrel or a pack of joggers). Have your dog checked by a veterinarian before significantly increasing her activity level.

🐾 Weather

Hot humid summers do dogs no favors. With no sweat glands and only panting available to disperse body heat, dogs are much more susceptible to heat stroke than we are. Unusually rapid panting and/or a bright red tongue are signs of heat exhaustion in your pet. Always carry enough water for your hike. Even the days that don't seem too warm can cause discomfort in dark-coated dogs if the sun is shining brightly. In cold weather, short-coated breeds may require additional attention.

🐾 Ticks

You won't be able to visit any of the Baltimore region's parks without encountering ticks. All are nasty but the deer tick - no bigger than a pin head - carries with it the spectre of Lyme disease. Lyme disease attacks a dog's joints and makes walking painful. The good news is that a tick needs to be embedded in the skin to transmit Lyme disease. It takes 4-6 hours for a tick to become embedded and another 24-48 hours to transmit Lyme disease bacteria.

When hiking, walk in the middle of trails away from tall grass and bushes. If your walk includes fields, consider long sleeves and long pants tucked into high socks. Wear a hat - ticks like hair. By checking your dog - and yourself - thoroughly after each walk you can help avoid Lyme disease. Ticks tend to congregate on your dog's ears, between the toes and around the neck and head.

🐾 Other Trail Hazards

Dogs won't get poison ivy but they can transfer it to you. Stinging nettle is a nuisance plant that lurks on the side of many trails and the slightest brush will deliver troublesome needles into a dog's coat. Some trails are littered with small pieces of broken glass that can slice a dog's paws. Nasty thorns can also blanket trails that we in shoes never notice.

🐾 Water

Surface water, including fast-flowing streams, is likely to be infested with a microscopic protozoa called *Girdia*, waiting to wreak havoc on a dog's intestinal system. The most common symptom is crippling diarrhea. Algae, pollutants and contaminants can all be in streams, ponds and puddles. If possible, carry fresh water for your dog on the trail - your dog can even learn to drink happily from a squirt bottle.

Outfitting The Dog For A Hike

These are the basics for taking your dog on a hike:

- **Collar**. It should not be so loose as to come off but you should be able to slide your flat hand under collar.

- **Identification Tags**.

- **Bandanna**. Can help distinguish your dog from game in hunting season.

- **Leash**. Leather lasts forever but if there's water in your dog's future, consider quick-drying nylon.

- **Water**. Carry 8 ounces for every hour of hiking.

🐾 I want my dog to help carry water, snacks and other supplies on the trail. How do I choose a dog pack?

To select an appropriate dog pack measure your dog's girth around the rib cage to determine the best pack size. A dog pack should fit securely without hindering the dog's ability to walk normally.

🐾 How does a dog wear a pack?

The pack, typically with cargo pouches on either side, should ride as close to the shoulders as possible without limiting movement. The straps that hold the dog pack in place should be situated where they will not cause chafing.

🐾 Will my dog wear a pack?

Wearing a dog pack is no more obtrusive than wearing a collar, although some dogs will take to a pack easier than others. Introduce the pack by draping a towel over your dog's back in the house and then having him wear an empty pack on short walks. Progressively add some crumpled newspaper and then bits of clothing. Fill the pack with treats and reward your dog from the stash. Soon he will associate the dog pack with an outdoor adventure and will eagerly look forward to wearing it.

🐾   How much weight can I put into a dog pack?

Many dog packs are sold by weight recommendations. A healthy, well-conditioned dog can comfortably carry 25% to 33% of its body weight. Breeds prone to back problems or hip dysplasia should not wear dog packs. Consult your veterinarian before stuffing the pouches with gear.

🐾   What are good things to put in a dog pack?

Low density items such as food and poop bags are good choices. Ice cold bottles of water can cool your dog down on hot days. Don't put anything in a dog pack that can break. Dogs will bang the pack on rocks and trees when they wiggle through tight spots in the trail. Dogs also like to lie down in creeks and other wet spots so seal items in plastic bags. A good use for dog packs on day hikes around Baltimore is trail maintenance - your dog can pack out trash left by inconsiderate visitors before you.

🐾   Are dog booties a good idea?

Dog booties can be an asset, especially for the occasional canine hiker whose paw pads have not become toughened. Many trails, especially hillside routes, involve rocky terrain. In some places, broken glass abounds. Hiking boots for dogs are designed to prevent pads from cracking while trotting across rough surfaces. Used in winter, dog booties provide warmth and keep ice balls from forming between toe pads when hiking through snow.

🐾   What should a doggie first aid kit include?

Even when taking short hikes it is a good idea to have some basics available for emergencies:

- 4" square gauze pads
- cling type bandaging tapes
- topical wound disinfectant cream
- tweezers
- petroleum jelly (to cover ticks)
- veterinarian's phone number

Low Impact Hiking With Your Dog

Everytime you hike with your dog on the trail you are an ambassador for all dog owners. Some people you meet won't believe in your right to take a dog on the trail. Be friendly to all and make the best impression you can by practicing low impact hiking with your dog:

- Pack out everything you pack in.

- Do not leave dog scat on the trail; if you haven't brought plastic bags for poop removal bury it away from the trail and topical water sources.

- Hike only where dogs are allowed.

- Stay on the trail.

- Do not allow your dog to chase wildlife.

- Step off the trail and wait with your dog while horses and other hikers pass.

- Do not allow your dog to bark - people are enjoying the trail for serenity.

- Have as much fun on your hike as your dog does.

The Other End Of The Leash

Leash laws are like speed limits - everyone seems to have a private interpretation of their validity. Some dog owners never go outside with an unleashed dog; others treat the laws as suggestions or disregard them completely. It is not the purpose of this book to tell dog owners where to go to evade the leash laws or reveal the parks where rangers will look the other way at an unleashed dog. Nor is it the business of this book to preach vigilant adherence to the leash laws. Nothing written in a book is going to change people's behavior with regard to leash laws. So this will be the last time leash laws are mentioned, save when we point out the parks where dogs are permitted off leash. Suffice to say that throughout the Baltimore region, dogs are universally required by law to be on leash at all times.

The Best of the Best...

The 10 Best Places To Hike With Your Dog In Greater Baltimore

Blue Ribbon - Robert E. Lee Park (Baltimore County)

With its rough-around-the-edges look, Robert E. Lee radiates plenty of canine charm. It feels as if dogs are welcome here and the 456-acre park has evolved into a prime destination for dog walkers of all sorts. Looking for a quick walk and a swim? Lake Roland can't be beat for deep water dog paddling. After a half-day's outing with your dog on the hiking trails? Cross the light rail line and the trail system explodes into a maze of hard-packed dirt passageways through the woods. Just need to let the dog romp with some buddies? Robert E. Lee Park may as well be Rover E. Lee Park. You'll find more dogs per hour here than any park in the Baltimore area.

#2 - Gunpowder Falls State Park - Hereford (Baltimore County)

At Hereford the canine hiker can find any length or type of hike to set tails wagging. Long out-and-back walks through a rugged gorge (this is Baltimore?) can be combined with many side trails that scamper up the valley slopes. You'll find plenty of great canine swimming holes in the river, fed by outflows from the Prettyboy Dam. You can even take the dog right to the base of the dam on a narrow trail drenched in mountain laurel.

#3 - Susquehanna State Park (Harford County)

The first European to set eyes on the Susquehanna River was English explorer John Smith. He was suitably impressed. "Heaven and earth," he wrote, "seemed never to have agreed better to frame a place for man's commodious and delightful habitation." Dog owners might readily concur. At Susquehanna State Park you can test trails in the hills that will leave man and dog panting or stroll along the shady Susquehanna and Tidewater Canal towpath, as level and pleasant an excursion as you can take with your dog.

#4 - Downs Memorial Park (Anne Arundel County)

Looking for a dog-friendly park? At Downs Memorial Park there is a "pet parking" stall outside the information center. A dog drinking bowl is chained to a human water fountain. The walking is fine too. Some five miles of easy hiking through woodlands of oak and maple and holly and gum. Best of all is Dog Beach, an isolated, scruffy 40-yard stretch of sand where you can let the dog off leash for canine aquatics in the Chesapeake Bay. The wave action is just right for dogs and there is enough sand for digging. Need we say more?

#5 - Gunpowder Falls State Park - Sweet Air (Baltimore/Harford County)

Sweet Air offers more than 12 miles of well-marked rambles on four main trails and several connector branches. Unlike other sections of Gunpowder Falls State Park, the water is not the star at Sweet Air. Rather the attraction is a pastiche of open fields (still under cultivation) and wooded landscapes on either side of the river. Don't forget to check out the farm ponds on the property for some canine refreshment.

#6 - Oregon Ridge Park (Baltimore County)

Save for the demanding rocky slopes of the S. James Campbell Trail, the hiking on Oregon Ridge's six miles of trails is almost uniformly wide and soft to the paw. The folks at Oregon Ridge are accommodating to dog owners - if you forget the leash they will loan you one. There are many trail options in this 1000-acre park and don't be afraid to learn something here. An interpretive trail leads to exhibits on the bountiful natural resources that made Oregon Ridge an active mining community in the 19th century: water, timber, iron and marble.

#7 - Gunpowder Falls State Park - Bel Air (Baltimore County)

From the parking lot on US 1 there are hours of hiking on both sides of the Gunpowder Falls in either direction. The highlight for canine hikers here is the Sweathouse Branch Wildlands Area that provides some of the best loop trails in the Gunpowder Falls state park system. The healthy hill climbs and wide trails give a big feel to this 5.1-mile walk as it meanders through differing forest types. Continue just past the end of the Sweathouse Trail to the Long Green Run and you'll find one of the best canine swimming holes in Greater Baltimore. Racing water is funnelled into a deep pool by a whale-shaped rock that serves as a natural diving board for playful dogs.

#8 - Patapsco Valley State Park (Carroll, Howard and Baltimore counties)

Dogs are banned in most areas of Maryland's first state park, established in 1907. But there is plenty of lemonade to be squeezed from those lemons served up by the state of Maryland. Dogs are welcomed in undeveloped areas such as Feezer's Lane where a short hike leads to the base of Liberty Dam; Henryton Road which sports a wild and wooly streamside adventure; access to the tamed Patapsco River at historic Daniels; and breathtaking views of the river valley from Buzzard's Rock off Hilltop Road.

#9 - Savage Park (Howard County)

Three unconnected areas surrounding the confluence of the Middle Patuxent and Little Patuxent rivers conspire to form Savage Park. The Wincopin Neck Trails are the prime destination for the canine hiker where most of the walking is level except where the paths plunge to the edge of the rivers. Across the water, the Savage Historic Mill Trail is a wide, level wooded path that traces the boulder-pocked stream below the confluence for 3/4 mile. Pools in the falls are the prettiest canine swimming holes in Greater Baltimore.

#10 - Soldiers Delight Natural Environmental Area (Baltimore County)

Soldier's Delight is the ideal change-up from the tall trees and rushing streams found at most Baltimore area parks. Keep your eyes open as you wander through Soldier's Delight's 2700 acres. The lack of nutrients in the soil of these "barrens" produce a prairie-like environment loaded with rare insects, rocks and more than three dozen endangered plant species. The distinctive green-tinted serpentine stone sticks up through the thin soil, however, and, while easy on the eye, can be tough on the paw.

"A door is what a dog is perpetually on the wrong side of."
- James Thurber

The 10 Best Trails To Hike With Your Dog In Greater Baltimore For Less Than One Hour

There are many great places to walk your dog around Baltimore. But what if you only had one hour to walk one trail with your dog, where would you go? Here are ten candidates for the perfect dog walking experience on a time budget:

(1) **Camel's Den Trail** (Patapsco Valley State Park, Daniels Area, Howard County)

On this loop you will enjoy the flattest dogwalking in greater Baltimore or some of the steepest. A hiking loop begins just across the small stream by the parking lot; to the left the trail switchbacks to the top of a high ridge leading past the Camel's Den cave and to the right it begins a 2.5-mile journey on a former railbed of the Baltimore & Ohio Railroad. The two are joined by an old access road. Backed up by the Daniels Dam, the dog paddling in the Patapsco River is super here.

(2) **Circle Trail** (Cylburn Arboretum, Baltimore County)

The 176 acres of Cylburn Arboretum's grounds are visited by five loop trails, all of which can be reached from the Circle Trail. This is a paw-pleasing circumnavigation on a wide path of soft dirt or cedar mulch but you will still want to stray off the trail to read the labels of the many ornamental trees.

(3) **Gunpowder South Trail** (Gunpowder Falls State Park, Hereford Area, Baltimore County)

The entire length of this scenic route is 7.1 miles but with only one hour you'll just cover the western section of the trail from Falls Road to Prettyboy Dam (named for a local farmer's favorite horse who drowned in a nearby stream). This waterside path is narrow and requires a fair amount of rock scrambling for you and the dog in stretches. Your reward is stunning views of the rugged gorge.

(4) **Hashawha Trails** (Bear Creek Nature Center, Carroll County)

The blue-green (Vista-Stream) circuit totals a bit less than three miles, mostly on gently sloping ground. The Vista Trail takes in fields, woods and ponds. Toss in the Stream Trail (green blazes) and you add a restored log cabin, grassy meadows, the gurgling Bear Branch Creek and a boardwalk crossing over part of tranquil Lake Hashawha.

(5) **Hemlock Gorge** (Prettyboy Reservoir, Baltimore County)

The best hiking at Prettyboy is out of sight of the reservoir and along the Gunpowder Falls, accessed by pull-offs on Gunpowder Road. Here you'll find walks through dense hemlock forests, none more special than the hike back in time down Hemlock Gorge. For this one, leave the fire roads behind and walk down a narrow dirt path on the northeast side of the bridge over the river. After crossing a tumbling stream the towering hemlocks begin in earnest, blocking out all other plants except the mosses clinging to the rock outcroppings on the steep slopes. When the river bends 90 degrees to the right, it serves up one lasting impression of Hemlock Gorge before the civilized part of the trail comes to an end. Scarcely, a half-mile long, there is a fair amount of rock scrambling and log-hopping for a fairly robust dog to follow the river.

(6) **Loggers Red Trail** (Oregon Ridge Park, Baltimore County)

After you get under way with a pleasant stroll across the wooden bridge spanning the Grand Canyon of Oregon Ridge (an abandoned open pit mine), the shaded trail pulls you to the top of the ridge - elevated enough to launch hang gliders. The old access road makes for easy hiking. Along the way you can pick and choose from many short trails radiating off the red trail.

(7) **The Lower Susquehanna Heritage Greenways Trail** (Susquehanna State Park, Harford County)

Tracing the route of the 160-year old Susquehanna and Tidewater Canal towpath, this wide dirt path stretches 2.2 shady miles along the water. The level going makes for as pleasant a hike as you can take with your dog. Scan the skies beneath the Conowingo Dam for bald eagles plying the waters for an easy meal of stunned and splattered fish.

(8) **Savage Historic Mill Trail** (Savage Park, Howard County)

Starting with a stroll across the historic Bollman Truss Bridge, this wide, level wooded path traces the boulder-packed stream below the confluence of the Little and Middle Patuxent rivers for 3/4 mile. You will want to linger by the rushing water while your dog explores some of the prettiest canine swimming holes in the Baltimore area.

(9) **Serpentine Trail** (Soldiers Delight NEA, Baltimore County)

Early settlers called the region "barrens" because serpentine rock, colored green by the mineral olivine, was so close to the surface that every shovel seemed to clank against it and no crops would grow here. The hiking through rare grasses and stunted pines is more akin to midwestern prairies than Eastern woodlands in this unique habitat. Be careful of that serpentine stone on your dog's paws - it sticks out like the serrated edges of a knife in places.

(10) **White Trail** (Rocks State Park, Harford County)

This hardy loop trail runs up and down and around the mountainous knob. A short detour will lead you - and a well-tethered dog - to the top of the signature King and Queen's Throne rocks for an impressive view of Deer Creek. The trail will get narrow and rocky at times, conjuring up a true alpine feel to the walk.

13 Cool Things To See On Baltimore Trails With Your Dog

"If your dog is fat," the old saying goes, "you aren't getting enough exercise." But walking the dog need not be just about a little exercise. Here are 13 cool things you can see in greater Baltimore while out walking the dog.

AIRPLANES. The BWI Airport is the only airport in America that features a recreational trail. The Thomas A. Dixon Jr. Aircraft Observation Area on this 12.5-mile paved trail, opened in 1994, provides an ideal spot to watch the planes land directly in front of you. You won't be able to see the rubber hit the ground here but can see it from other spots along the trail. To get the feel of a big jet soaring directly over your head walk down a half-mile to the east (you'll see stop signs) and stand here. It won't be only jets using the airport either - you can spot an occasional propeller plane as well.

AMUSEMENT PARK RUINS. Although only 20 acres in size, the Bay Shore Park was considered one of the finest amusement parks ever built along the Chesapeake Bay. Built in 1906, the park featured an Edwardian-style dance hall, bowling alley and restaurant set among gardens and curving pathways. There were rides such as a water toboggan and Sea Swing. Visitors would come out from Baltimore on a trolley line. Most of the park was torn down after its closure in 1947 but you and the dog can explore the remains of the turn-of-the-century amusement park, including the wood-framed trolley station and the restored ornamental fountain, in North Shore State Park. Complete your tour with a hike down the old Bayshore Pier which juts almost a quarter-mile into the wind-swept Bay - a diving board once operated here where benches are today.

BALD EAGLES.   With nearly 13,000 acres of undeveloped space, the Patuxent Research Refuge is said to be the largest patch of green space remaining on the East Coast between Boston and Raleigh. Research done here was used by Rachel Carson to argue that the pesticide DDT was weakening the shells of bird eggs, especially bald eagles, causing them not to hatch. Her book, *Silent Spring*, led to the banning of DDT and launched the modern environmental movement. Today more than 250 species - 8 of every 10 birds that can be seen in the Baltimore area - have been sighted at Patuxent, including a pair of nesting bald eagles in the North Tract in Anne Arundel County. These representatives of America's national symbol quite possibly could be the bald eagles living closest to the White House. Don't let your dog dig around at the North Tract - this land was once a testing ground for Fort Meade and may still harbor live ammunition.

If you aren't lucky enough to spot the eagles in flight at the refuge, try hiking the Hashawha Trails at the Bear Branch Nature Center in Carroll County. Here is the chance for your curious dog to look a bald eagle in the eye. The Nature Center maintains a M.A.S.H. unit for raptors who have been injured too badly to be returned to the wild. The cages for eagles, kestrels, hawks, owls, turkey vultures and other recovering birds of prey are on the Vista Trail.

CANAL LOCK.   Near North Park in Havre de Grace, the 444-mile Susquehanna River is busy emptying 19 million gallons of fresh water every minute into the Chesapeake Bay that it has drained from 13 million acres of land. The rocky river upstream from here, however, is not navigable and the 45-mile Susquehanna and Tidewater Canal opened for barges, pulled at 4 miles per hour by mules, to haul goods between Havre de Grace and Wrightsville, Pennsylvania. The first of 29 locks operated here and it has been restored to its original appearance including a pivoting footbridge that swung open to allow barge traffic to pass. The handsome brick Lock House, now a museum open on weekends, dates to the canal's opening in 1840. The large grassy lawn can be used for a first-rate game of fetch.

CHOATE MINE.   The first chromium mines in America were opened in rural Baltimore County in 1808 and from 1828 to 1850 just about every scrap of chrome in the world came from here. Along the Choate Mine Trail in Soldiers Delight Natural Environmental Area you can stand in front of the entrance to the Choate Mine and look into the slanting hole kept open by half-timbered posts. So close the cool air will rustle your dog's fur. The mine once ran 200 feet deep and 160 feet across.

DAMS.   After a long hike at Robert E. Lee Park around Lake Roland you can sit on top of the Greek Revival valve house completed in 1862 and look over the stone dam. Lake Roland, created after plugging up Jones Falls, was Baltimore's first reservoir. This smallish dam is just an appetizer for the dams yet to come that were built to quench Baltimore's thirst. Others to see include hiking to the base of Liberty Dam at the end of Feezer's Lane in Patapsco State Park or using the Gunpowder South Trail in the Hereford section of Gunpowder Falls State Park to see the Prettyboy Dam, built in 1933. No tour of Baltimore's dams would be complete without a visit to Conowingo Dam, America's longest concrete slab dam across the Susquehanna River. You can take the dog to gaze out at the Conowingo Dam in Susquehanna State Park.

FORTS.   At Fort Howard Park your dog can climb into an actual gun battery and scan the Patapsco River just like gunnery officers who once aimed guns capable of accurately firing 1,000 pound projectiles eight miles. Ruins abound at the former "Bulldog at Baltimore's Gate," including remainders left over from the 1960s when a mock Vietnamese village was created for training at Fort Howard. Batteries and magazines that once formed the coastal defense of Baltimore in 1899 can also be seen at Fort Armistead Park and Fort Smallwood Park. As for Baltimore's most famous fort, dogs are also welcome at

Fort McHenry National Monument. Unlike the others, your best friend won't be able to explore the actual fort but there is plenty of fresh grass to romp on outside the bastion walls.

HENRYTON TUNNEL.   The Baltimore & Ohio Railroad built its first line west along the Patapsco River and the trails at Henryton Road in Patapsco State Park follow a particularly historic stretch of the Old Main Line. On a rainy night in 1830 Irish laborers, tired of waiting for back pay, rioted and managed to destroy all this track for five miles to Sykesville. The disturbance prompted the first ever American troop transport by train when the Baltimore militia rode out to squelch the rampage. When the trail crosses this section of railroad track look to the west and see the Henryton Tunnel. Opened in 1850, it is the second-oldest tunnel in the world that remains in active railroad use.

MODEL TRAINS.   Thomas Winans made his fortune building the Russian transcontinental railroad for Czar Nicholas I. He learned railroading from his father Ross who invented the swivel wheel truck that enabled trains to negotiate curves. Their railroad heritage is preserved at Leakin Park in Baltimore by the Chesapeake & Allegheny Live Steamers who maintain three miles of track for miniature steam trains that carry passengers (sorry, no dogs) free of charge the second Sunday of every month. Capable of speeds of 25 mph, the trains rumble along instead at a passenger-friendly 6 mph.

MODERN ART. The natural beauty of Quiet Waters Park in Annapolis is augmented by the outdoor sculptures that grace the grounds. Sculptures are chosen by jury from national and international artists working with a variety of material and installed on a rotating basis. When your dog tires of sniffing the statuary, you can take her to Anne Arundel County's first dog park at the back of Quiet Waters. Not only are there two large fenced-in enclosures for big and small dogs but there is a dog beach on the South River for serious dog paddling.

POT ROCKS. From the parking lot on US 1 at the Big Gunpowder Falls there is great canine hiking on both sides of the river in either direction. On the opposite bank heading downstream on the Big Gunpowder Trail, about a mile down, are the Pot Rocks. You and the dog can walk out and examine the conical depressions created in the bedrock by swirling waters armed with millions of years worth of grinding cobbles. These unique potholes can be a foot or more deep. Keep hiking another two miles down the river and you reach the last series of rapids on the Gunpowder as the water leaves the hilly Piedmont region and slips into the flat Coastal Plain.

RARE TREES. Growing unobtrusivley beside the parking lot at Tridelphia Recreation Area is one of the rarest native ornamental trees in the world, the *Franklinia Alatamaha*. A relative of the camelia, this flowering tree is prized at any time of the year - in the winter for its striped bark, in the summer for its palm-sized snow white flowers, and in the fall for its deep red leaves. The Franklinia was discovered by Philadelphia botanist John Bartram in 1765 in a remote corner of Georgia along the Alatamaha River and named for his friend Benjamin Franklin. It has not been found growing in the wild since 1790.

For a true arboreal education however, treat the dog to Cylburn Arboretum in Baltimore, one of the few such tree museums that permit dogs on the grounds. The collection at Cylburn features several Maryland Big Tree Champions including an Italian maple and a paperback maple. Two easy champions to see are on the lawn in the right front of the mansion: a castor aralia with large glossy leaves and an Amur maackia. Both trees are native to Asia and are resilient to pests. The maackia is a member of the pea family discovered by 19th century explorer Karlovich Maack along the Amur River between Siberia and China.

UNUSUAL BRIDGES. Hiking in Gunpowder Falls State Park in Harford County, downstream from Jerusalem Mill about 1/2 mile, is Jericho Covered Bridge, one of only six remaining covered bridges in Maryland and the only one of its kind in Baltimore and Harford counties. Old folk wisdom held that these bridges were built to resemble a barn so as to entice a wary horse across water but the bridges are covered simply to protect the expensive wooden decks. The ford at this point across the Little Gunpowder Falls dates to Colonial times; the bridge was constructed in 1865. Builder Thomas F. used three truss types in its construction: the simple Multiple King Post; the horizontal Queen Post extension; and the Burr Arch, patented in 1804 by Theodore Burr, for stability. Renovated in 1981, the Jericho Covered Bridge still carries traffic.

In Howard County's Savage Park, on Foundry Road at the trailhead for the Historic Mill Trail, is the last remaining Bollman Truss bridge in the world. Your dog can trot across the first successful iron bridge used by railroads, patented by Wendell A. Bolman in 1852. This example, a National Historic Civil Engineering Landmark, originally carried traffic on the Baltimore & Ohio main line but was disassembled and put into service here for Savage Mill in 1887.

The 50 Best Places To Hike With Your Dog In The Baltimore Region

1
Robert E. Lee Park

The Park

Lake Roland was created in 1862 as Baltimore's first city water reservoir, eventually named for Roland Run, a feeder stream from the north that got *its* name from 17th- century settler Roland Thornberry. The water system was abandoned in 1915 due to silting in the lake. In the 1940s the 456-acre property was converted into a Baltimore city park (although outside the city limits) using funds bequeathed to the city for a statue honoring Confederate General Robert E. Lee.

Baltimore County

Distance from the Beltway
 - 3 miles from Exit 23
Phone Number
 - None
Website
 - None
Admission Fee
 - None
Directions
 - The park is just north of Baltimore and run by the city. The obscured entrance to Robert E. Lee Park is on Lakeside Drive off Falls Road (MD 25), just north of Lake Avenue.

The Walks

Robert E. Lee Park lacks a public entrance, has no signage, no amenities - in short, a perfect place to take a dog. And you will see more dogs per hour here than anywhere in Baltimore. Improvements will mean more visitation and more restrictions on dogs. Until that time, however, Robert E. Lee can provide just about any type of outing you want with your dog.

Interested in a quick walk with a swim? Circle the old Lakeside Park loop above the Lake Roland dam. Looking for a long, solitary hike? Cross the light rail line and explore a maze of hard-packed dirt trails through the woods. Some push into marshy areas along the lake for a bit of Baltimore's best bird watching. Warblers, ducks, geese and herons ply the reed-choked wetlands. Desire a walk around a lake? Cut across the lake on a narrow path beside the rail line (not for skittery dogs - a passing train will be only a

> **Bonus**
> After a long hike at Lake Roland you can sit on top of the Greek Revival valve house completed in 1862 and look over the stone dam. Lake Roland was created after plugging up Jones Falls.

few unfenced feet from the trail) and pick up a rollercoaster lakeside path across Lake Roland. Your dog will delight in bounding up the short slopes in happy anticipation of what the other side holds.

Trail Sense: There are no wayfinding aids whatsoever in Robert E. Lee Park.

Dog Friendliness

As dog-friendly a municipal park as a dog owner is likely to find, Robert E. Lee is the unoffical Baltimore dog park.

Traffic

Bikes are allowed on the trails but are far outnumbered by dogs.

Canine Swimming

There are many great places for a canine swim in Lake Roland on the dam side of the railroad bridge; across the tracks access to the lake is more limited. Look for a dip in the wide, but shallow, Jones Falls over here.

Trail Time

More than an hour.

> *"The greatest pleasure of a dog is that you may make a fool of yourself with him, and not only will he not scold you, but will make a fool of himself too."*
> — Samuel Butler

2
Gunpowder Falls State Park - Hereford

The Park

Gunpowder Falls State Park embraces more than 17,000 acres of property in distinct tracts from the Maryland-Pennsylvania state line to the Chesapeake Bay. The Hereford Area on the Big Gunpowder River preserves 3,620 acres of pristine Maryland woodlands. Located where rivers tumble down the fall line of the Piedmont Plateau to the flat Coastal Plain, there was plenty of water power here to drive the industry of a young America. Ruins of these mills, including a gunpowder mill which exploded on the Panther Branch on July 7, 1874, can still be seen in the park.

Baltimore County

Distance from the Beltway
 - 13 miles from Exit 24
Phone Number
 - (410) 592-2897
Website
 - http:/www.dnr.state.md.us/publiclands/hereford.html
Admission Fee
 - None
Directions
 - The park is near the town of Hereford, one of the county's oldest. Take Exit 27 off I-83 onto Mt. Carmel Road. The main lot is at the end of Bunker Hill Road off York Road. Other trailheads are on Mt. Carmel, York, Masemore, Falls and Big Falls roads.

The Walks

At Hereford the canine hiker can find any length or type of hike to set tails wagging. The marquee trail among 20 miles of hiking is the 7.1-mile Gunpowder South Trail that includes bites of trail more reminiscent of West Virginia than Baltimore, especially the western segment from Falls Road to Prettyboy Dam. While most of the narrow dirt trails at Hereford are easy on the paw, this waterside path is rocky and requires a fair amount of rock scrambling. Your reward is stunning views of the rugged gorge. Walking along the South Trail, and its companion North Trail on the opposite bank, is generally level as it follows the

> **Bonus**
> The Gunpowder South Trail continues past the park boundaries to the base of the Prettyboy Dam where you can watch water releases from the reservoir. This water blasts out from the bottom of the lake providing a steady supply of chilled water favored by trout and the Big Gunpowder Falls is a nationally recognized trout stream.

meanderings of the stream.

For hearty climbers, look to the many side trails which can be wedded to the South Trail to form several loops of between one and two miles of length.

Trail Sense: The South Trail is blazed in white and most side trails are blazed in blue. Equestrian trails are blazed yellow. Trail maps are available but not on site; consult the mapboard in the York Road parking lot in the middle of the park.

Dog Friendliness

Dogs are allowed on all the trails but not in the campground at Camp Wood.

Traffic

Most of the traffic you see will be out in the river.

Canine Swimming

Although limited by high banks, fisherman and watercraft, there are plenty of great pools in the Big Gunpowder Falls. Two of Katie's favorites are at the confluence of the Panther Branch and the Big Gunpowder and beneath an imposing outcropping just downstream from Raven Falls.

Trail Time

More than an hour.

3
Susquehanna State Park

The Park

The first European to set eyes on the Susquehanna River was English explorer John Smith. He was suitably impressed. "Heaven and earth seemed never to have agreed better to frame a place for man's commodious and delightful habitation," he wrote. While sailing in this area, Smith met the native Susquehannocks, who gave the river, the longest of any waterway on the East Coast, its name. Industry came early to the area - the Lapidium community in the park traces its beginnings to 1683 and the park's restored Rock Run Grist Mill dates to 1794. The water-powered mill grinds corn into meal on summer weekends. Today Susquehanna State Park, opened in 1965, encompasses 2,500 inviting acres.

Harford County

Distance from the Beltway
 - 25 miles from Exit 33
Phone Number
 - (410) 557-7994
Website
 - www.dnr.state.md.us/publiclands/central/susquehanna.html
Admission Fee
 - There is a $2 admission to the private Steppingstone Museum in the park.
Directions
 - The park is 3 miles northwest of Havre de Grace. Take I-95 to Route 155, exit 89. Go west on Route 155 to Route 161. Turn right and right again on Rock Run Road to the park.

The Walks

Susquehanna State Park is a winning combination of history, scenery and wildlife. The well-maintained trails are short enough to complete and challenging without being exhausting. The abundance of large rocks in the Susquehanna River enables you to sit out in the water while your dog splashes around you. Among its 15 miles of trails the park features several loop trails in the hills above the Susquehanna River Valley. Most are around two miles in distance. If using the green-blazed Deer Creek Trail be on the look-

> **Bonus**
> The chance to see bald eagles, especially in the winter. The great piscavorious birds favor massive nests in the 100-foot treetops along the banks of the Susquehanna River from which they dive and pluck stunned and splattered fish from the spillways beneath the Conowingo Dam, America's longest concrete-slab dam. Wading birds are always on display.

out for a magnificent spreading white oak in the middle of the walk. Be aware that there are few streams on the slopes to refresh your dog on a hot day.

The Lower Susquehanna Heritage Greenways Trail, which connects the park at Deer Creek with the Conowingo Dam is as pleasant a hike as you can take with your dog. Tracing the route of the 160-year old Susquehanna and Tidewater Canal towpath, the wide dirt path stretches 2.2 shaded miles along the water.

Trail Sense: The trails are well-blazed and easy to follow. A detailed trail map is also available.

Dog Friendliness

Dogs are permitted everywhere in the park, including the campground, except the Deer Creek picnic area.

Traffic

The Susquehanna trails are popular with mountain bikers and equestrians but it is easy to find solitude, especially in the hills.

Canine Swimming

The rock-strewn Susquehanna is full of clear pools for your dog to paddle around in with many points of access from the trail. Be alert for water releases from the Conowingo Dam, however, which make the lower Susquehanna rise dangerously.

Trail Time

More than an hour.

4
Downs Memorial Park

The Park
In the early days of English settlement Bodkin Neck was the property of land speculators. It came under cultivation in 1828 when Henry Dunbar purchased most of the peninsula. The land that would become Downs Park was lumbered until the mid-1800s and eventually cultivated to grow vegetables on Deer Park Farm. In 1913 the property was purchased by H.R. Mayo Thom who converted his now Rocky Beach Farm - named for the red sandstone thrusting out of the sandy beach - into a gentleman's summer estate.

Anne Arundel County

Distance from the Beltway
- 12.5 miles from Exit 2
Phone Number
- (410) 222-6230
Website
- http://web.aacpl.lib.md.us/rp/parks/dp/
Admission Fee
- There is a $4 daily vehicle charge; closed on Tuesdays
Directions
- Downs Park is in Pasadena. Take Pinehurst Road off Mountain Road (MD 177).

The Walks
A paved perimeter trail loops 3.6 miles around the Downs Park property. Most of the twisting route is easy hiking through woodlands of oak and maple and holly and gum. There are another three miles of unpaved trails through the Natural Area, including an eco-trail with interpretive sites. Many of these natural paths are old farm roads - wide and soft under paw.

Trail Sense: A park map is available and the trails are well-marked.

Dog Friendliness
Downs Park is one of the most dog-friendly parks in greater Baltimore. A dog drinking bowl is chained to a water fountain and there is a "pet parking" stall outside the Information Center.

> **Bonus**
> At the South Overlook is an osprey nesting platform to observe the activities of the fish-hunting hawk. Although preferring a flat-topped tree, ospreys will happily choose man-made structures such as these for homes. Out on the water, an osprey will hover above the surface looking for a fish before striking with talons extended. An adult bird will succeed one time in four with this maneuver. There is also an aviary and raptor pen for up-close viewing of these striking carniviverous birds.

Dogs are not allowed to walk through the formal Mother's Garden.

Traffic
The trails in the Natural Area are less crowded than the active recreation sections of the park.

Canine Swimming
Behind the North Overlook is an isolated, scruffy 40-yard stretch of sand known as Dog Beach just for canine aquatics. There is excellent wave action from the Chesapeake Bay and enough sand for digging. For less adventurous dogs there is swimming in a quiet pond adjacent to Dog Beach.

Trail Time
More than an hour.

5
Gunpowder Falls State Park - Sweet Air

Balt/Harford Counties

Distance from the Beltway
- 14 miles from Exit 31

Phone Number
- (410) 557-7994

Website
- http://www.dnr.state.md.uspubliclands/ central/ gunpowder.html

Admission Fee
- None

Directions
- The Sweet Air section is east of Jacksonville. From Sweet Air Road (MD 145) turn onto Greene Road and make a left on Moores Road to park entrance.

The Park

Unlike other sections of Gunpowder Falls State Park, the water is not the star at Sweet Air. Only a short segment of the trail system follows the Little Gunpowder Falls, which flows thinly near its headwaters at this point. The attraction at Sweet Air is a patchwork of open fields (still under cultivation) and wooded landscapes on either side of the river.

The Walks

Sweet Air offers more than twelve miles of well-marked rambles on four main trails and several connector branches. The feature hike is the white-blazed Little Gunpowder Trail, serving up a buffet of Sweet Air splendors in the course of its 3.8 miles: upland farm fields, fern-encrusted hillsides and lush riparian forests. Short loops off this trail visit a quiet woodland pond and a small white pine plantation. Look for a cornucopia of trail surfaces - soft dirt, hard pack, wood chip and mowed grass.

A total exploration of Sweet Air will include the blue-blazed Boundary Trail which means wading through the Little Gunpowder to walk into Baltimore County. If this proves enjoyable, consider some of the rogue trails at Sweet Air near the water.

Trail Sense: A trail map is available but not on site. In addition to blazed routes there are signposts with "You Are Here" maps indicating shortcuts sprinkled on the trail system.

> **Bonus**
> Rest stops have been set up along the trails that give Sweet Air the feel of an English manor park, a good place to come and forget about time. One of the best is at a pretty stretch of riverwalk where a sycamore tree has grown horizontally inches above the water and its branches are growing vertically like a gove of slender trees.

Dog Friendliness
Dogs are permitted on the trails at Sweet Air.

Traffic
The trails are popular with equestrians and bikes are permitted but Sweet Air is blissfully uncrowded.

Canine Swimming
Gunpowder Falls is generally deep enough only for sustained splashing but the farm ponds on the property make for good dog paddling.

Trail Time
More than an hour.

"They are superior to human beings as companions. They do not quarrel or argue with you. They never talk about themselves but listen to you while you talk about yourself, and keep an appearance of being interested in the conversation."
- Jerome K. Jerome

6
Oregon Ridge Park

The Park

An active mining community thrived at Oregon Ridge in the mid-19th century. Irish immigrants and emancipated slaves did most of the hard work pulling first Geothite, containing iron ore, and then high-grade Cockeysville marble from the hills. The iron was smelted in a furnace along Oregon Branch and the marble was used to build the United States Capitol and the Washington Monument. The Oregon Ridge Iron Works supported a company town of 220 workers and their families before the business died away in the 1870s. Today Oregon Ridge Park is Baltimore County's largest park with more than 1000 acres of woods and meadows.

Baltimore County
Distance from the Beltway
- 7 miles from Exit 24
Phone Number
- (410) 887-1815
Website
- www.oregonridge.org
Admission Fee
- None
Directions
- Oregon Ridge Park is 2 miles west of Cockeysville. From I-83 take Exit 20B west on Shawan Road. After one mile make a left on Beaver Dam Road and immediately take right fork into the park.

The Walks

Although you get under way with a pleasant stroll into the forest across the wooden bridge spanning the Grand Canyon of Oregon Ridge (an abandoned open pit mine), it doesn't take long to realize you have signed on for a serious hike here. The Loggers Red Trail pulls you to the top of the ridge - elevated enough to launch hang gliders - and your pick of nine short trails. The full loop of the property leads south along the yellow trails and will add 4 stream crossings and serious hill climbs to your outing.

All told there are 6 miles of trails at Oregon Ridge. All are wooded and almost uniformly wide and soft to the paw. The lone

> **Bonus**
> An interpretive trail leads to exhibits on the bountiful natural resources that Oregon Ridge provided to settlers in the region: water, timber, iron, marble and rich farmland. The trail begins at recreated tenant houses of the Oregon Ridge Iron Works just below the Nature Center.

exception is the rocky slopes of the S. James Campbell Trail which are a trade-off for the scenic trekking in the ravine. Be sure to make your way to the half-mile Lake Trail, a rollicking romp above the green waters of the 45-foot deep Oregon Lake, a flooded old iron quarry.

Trail Sense: A trail map is available outside the Nature Center, the trails are well-marked and signposts at junctions alert you to new trailheads.

Dog Friendliness

Dogs are allowed throughout the Oregon Ridge Park trail system and if you've forgotten a leash you can borrow one in the Nature Center. Dogs are not permitted in the beach area at Oregon Lake.

Traffic

No horses or bikes are allowed on these trails.

Canine Swimming

Baisman Run is simply for splashing but Ivy Pond at the junction of the Ivy Hill and S. James Campbell trails is a delightful stop for a dip, ringed by fir trees and outcroppings of Loch Raven schist.

Trail Time

More than an hour.

7
Gunpowder Falls State Park - Belair Road

The Park
The fall line between the Piedmont and coastal plains occurs in this section of the park, just west of Route 40. Sloops could come up the Big Gunpowder Falls as far as this point to load shipments from the many mills operating upstream. A popular ferry once operated at Long Calm, the stretch of river west of today's I-95. The Marquis de Lafayette camped here famously during the American Revolution. Today the park's trails run for 8 miles along the Big Gunpowder Falls water chutes.

The Walks
The highlight for canine hikers here is the Sweathouse Branch Wildlands Area that provides some of the best loop trails in the Gunpowder park system. The outside loop links the Wildlands Trail (pink), the Stocksdale Trail (blue) and the Sweathouse Trail (yellow) and covers 5.1 miles. The healthy hill climbs and wide trails give a big feel to this walk as it meanders through differing forest types. These trails are rocky under paw at times.

On the east side of U.S. Route 1 the Lost Pond Trail runs in a 3.1-mile long lasso on its way to an abandoned mill pond. The yellow-blazed Sawmill Trail loops off this footpath into the hillside of the gorge to visit the ruins of the 1833 Carroll family

---

Baltimore County

Distance from the Beltway
 - 5 miles from Exit 32
Phone Number
 - (410) 557-7994
Website
 - http://www.dnr.state.md.uspubliclands/ central/ gunpowder.html
Admission Fee
 - None
Directions
 - The parking area and trailheads are on the northbound side of US 1 (Belair Road) after it crosses the Big Gunpowder Falls, about 5.4 miles north of the I-695 Beltway). Polar parking lots on the ends of the park are on the south side of the river on Harford Road (MD 147) and on Jones Road off the Pulaski Highway (US 40).

> **Bonus**
> In the center of the Big Gunpowder Falls, about 1.2 miles east of the parking lot, are the Pot Rocks. Best accessed from the Big Gunpowder Trail, you and the dog can walk out and examine the conical depressions created in the bed rock by swirling waters armed with millions of years worth of grinding cobbles. These unique potholes can be a foot or more deep.

sawmill. These trails require several stream crossings and are often muddy. For all-day hikers the Big Gunpowder Trail picks its way through the woods along the entire length of the river on the south bank, eventually reaching the last rapids of the Gunpowder. The narrow dirt trail is blazed white.

Trail Sense: A trail map is available at the main park office in Kingsville but not on site. Consult the mapboard in the parking lot to plan routes. The trails are extremely well-marked.

Dog Friendliness

Dogs are allowed on all these trails.

Traffic

Bicycles are banned from the Sweathouse Branch Wildlands Area. While popular, there are many more available miles of trail here than users.

Canine Swimming

Unless recent rains have been heavy, the dam-controlled Big Gunpowder Falls is often only deep enough only for splashing. But on Long Green Run, past the Sweathouse Trail, is one of the best canine swimming holes in the Baltimore area. Racing water is funnelled into a deep pool by a whale-shaped rock that serves as a natural diving board for playful dogs.

Trail Time

More than an hour.

8
Patapsco Valley State Park

The Park

Maryland's state park system began with the establishment of Patapsco State Forest Reserve in 1907. Today the park sprawls across 14,000 acres and four counties. The linear park traces the Patapsco River for 32 miles from southeastern Carroll County to tidewater in Baltimore Harbor.

The Walks

The widespread prohibitions against dogs in developed areas of Patapsco Valley State Park are a prime frustration for Baltimore dog owners. But there is plenty of lemonade to be squeezed from the lemons served up by the state of Maryland. Four undeveloped areas are recommended by the park service to take the dog:

Feezer's Lane (gravel road on west side of Marriottsville Road just north of the bridge over North Branch of Patapsco River). A narrow trail follows a high bank of the river for about a mile until it reaches a small stream crossing and opens into a burst of hiking opportunities in the Liberty Dam Reservoir. Straight ahead is the base of the Liberty Dam and a deep pool, to the right is a winding trek up a rocky old construction road (not recommended for soft paws) to a park at the top of the dam, to the left are miles of hilly, wooded equestrian trails.

Henryton Road (off MD 99 at the end of the road at the washed out bridge over South Branch Patapsco River). An unmarked fisherman's trail follows the stream for miles; it is particularly interesting to the east. The first part is wild and wooly with many

---

several counties

Distance from the Beltway
  - 3 miles from Exit 15
Phone Number
  - (410) 260-8835
Website
  - www.dnr.state.md.us/
  publiclands/central/
  patapscovalley.html
Admission Fee
  - only in developed areas
(where dogs are not permitted)
Directions
  - see The Walks

> **Bonus**
> The Baltimore & Ohio Railroad built its first line west along the Patapsco River and the trails at Henryton Road follow a particularly historic stretch of the Old Main Line. On a rainy night in 1830 Irish laborers, tired of waiting for back pay, rioted and managed to destroy all this track for 5 miles to Sykesville. The rampage prompted the first ever American troop transport by train when the Baltimore militia rode out to squelch the distubance. When the trail crosses this section of track look to the west at the Henryton Tunnel. Opened in 1850, it is the second-oldest tunnel in the world that remains in active railroad use. Look to the east and find a short concrete post by the side of the track. It is a vintage whistle post used to warn of the upcoming Marriottsville Road grade crossing around the bend. Few whistle posts survive today.

fallen trees to clamber over. The slopes are so littered with uprooted giants you may want to keep an eye out for any others about to tumble. Once across the railroad tracks the trail enters a flood plain and becomes buttery soft to the paw, beckoning you to continue. When you begin to hear vehicular traffic, turn around and head back. The best of this hike is over.

Daniels Area (at end of Daniels Road off Old Frederick Road, east of the intesection of Routes 29 and 99). Daniels was once a bustling mill village done in by shifting economics and flooding from Hurricane Agnes in 1972. You can enjoy either the flattest dogwalking in greater Baltimore or some of the steepest here. A hiking loop begins just across the small stream by the parking lot; to the left the trail switchbacks to the top of a high ridge past the Camel's Den cave and to the right it begins a 2.5-mile journey on a former railbed of the Baltimore & Ohio Railroad. After exploring the ridge for a mile the high trail drops down to the level riverside walk where you can complete the loop or turn left and follow as the old access road gives way to a single track dirt path. Behind the Daniels Dam, the Patapsco River is wide and still here, giving this walk a feel quite unlike any other in the region.

Hilltop Road at Hilton Area (off Frederick Road, Md 144, between Catonsville and Ellicott City). The state park actually offers up a pair of blazed hiking trails to ostracized dog owners in this section of Patapsco State Park above the Bloede Dam, the first hydropower dam to have electricty-producing turbines inside the dam. The Hilton Area is where John Glenn gave 43 acres of land to start the park nearly a century ago. The main trail at Hilltop is the yellow-blazed Buzzards Rock Trail, a 1.7-mile loop. The red-blazed Sawmill Branch Trail can also be used to complete the loop, but you will miss Buzzards Rock itself. This rocky promontory overlooks the tree-lined gorge where you can spot a gliding turkey vulture or just gauge how far you've climbed up or how far you have to go down. This trail up the cliff is steep, hard going but most of the walking through the mature forest at Hilltop or along the river is quite easy.

Trail Sense: These undeveloped areas are not on all park maps. Pick up the flyer *A Guide To Your Pet in Patapsco Valley State Park* for directions to dog-friendly hiking areas. Once there, the trails are generally not blazed.

Dog Friendliness

Dogs are only allowed in Patapsco State Park in undeveloped areas such as the ones described. Dogs are allowed in the campground at the Hollofield Area (only in about a dozen campsites) but can't leave the campsite.

Traffic

These undeveloped areas are not nearly as crowded as the popular people-only parts of Patapsco State Park.

Canine Swimming

There is great canine swimming in the Patapsco River in all four park areas save Feezer's Lane. As the Liberty Dam releases no water, this section of the river is all but dry. A deep pool at the base of the dam is tempting but difficult for the dog to access from the shore.

Trail Time

More than an hour.

As a young lawyer, 19th century Senator George Graham Vest of Missouri, addressed the jury on behalf of his client, suing a neighbor who had killed his dog. Vest's speech has come to be known as "Tribute to the Dog."

The best friend a man has in the world may turn against him and become his enemy. His son or daughter that he has reared with loving care may prove ungrateful. Those who are nearest and dearest to us, those whom we trust with our happiness and our good name may become traitors to their faith. The money that a man has, he may lose. It flies away from him, perhaps when he needs it most. A man's reputation may be sacrificed in a moment of ill-considered action. The people who are prone to fall on their knees to do us honor when success is with us may be the first to throw the stone of malice when failure settles its cloud upon our heads.

The one absolutely unselfish friend that man can have in this selfish world, the one that never deserts him, the one that never proves ungrateful or treacherous is his dog. A man's dog stands by him in prosperity and in poverty, in health and in sickness. He will sleep on the cold ground, where the wintry winds blow and the snow drives fiercely, if only he may be near his master's side. He will kiss the hand that has no food to offer; he will lick the wounds and sores that come in an encounter with the roughness of the world. He guards the sleep of his pauper master as if he were a prince. When all other friends desert, he remains. When riches take wings, and reputation falls to pieces, he is as constant in his love as the sun in its journey through the heavens.

If fortune drives the master forth an outcast in the world, friendless and homeless, the faithful dog asks no higher privilege than that of accompanying him, to guard him against danger, to fight against his enemies. And when the last scene of all comes, and death takes his master in its embrace and his body is laid away in the cold ground, no matter if all other friends pursue their way, there by the graveside will the noble dog be found, his head between his paws, his eyes sad, but open in alert watchfulness, faithful and true even in death.

9
Savage Park

The Park

Amos Williams and three brothers built a cotton works on the Patuxent River in 1822, naming it for John Savage, a director of the Bank of the United States who backed the project with $20,000. A major cloth producer for 125 years, the business declined rapidly after World War II due to a glut of canvas from returning war supplies and was gone by 1947. A visionary named Harry Heim bought the entire company town for $450,000 with dreams of a year-round Christmas village called Santa Heim, Merryland. Perhaps ahead of his time, the scheme suffered a quick death and the old mill was used mainly for warehouses until renovated for shops and offices and a park in 1988.

Howard County

Distance from the Beltway
- 13 miles from Exit 11
Phone Number
- (410) 313-4682
Website
- www.co.ho.md.us/rpsavage.html
Admission Fee
- None
Directions
- Savage Park is west of Savage, west of US 1. To reach the Wincopin Trails, exit US 1 to Guilford Road west. Make a left on Vollmerhausen Road to parking lot on left past schools. The Savage Loop is in town at the end of Baltimore Street. Parking for the Savage Mill Trail is on Foundry Street.

The Walks

Three unconnected areas surrounding the confluence of the Middle Patuxent and Little Patuxent rivers conspire to form Savage Park. Although the Wincopin Neck Trails are the prime destination of the canine hiker, you may want to warm up on the Savage Historic Mill Trail. This wide, level wooded path traces the boulder-pocked stream below the confluence for 3/4 of a mile. Pools in the falls are the prettiest canine swimming holes in the Baltimore region. Up the road are the hilly River Trail and

> **Bonus**
> On Foundry Road, at the trailhead for the Historic Mill Trail, is the last remaining Bollman Truss bridge in the world. Your dog can trot across the first successful iron bridge used by railroads, patented by Wendell A. Bolman in 1852. This example, a National Historic Civil Engineering Landmark, originally carried traffic on the B&O main line but was disassemble and put into service here for Savage Mill in 1887.

Lost Horse Trail behind the recreation area.

The main hiking routes at Wincopin Neck are the red-blazed Wincopin Trail and the green-blazed Beech Grove Trail. The Wincopin heads straight out from the parking lot before plunging downhill to loop around Hogs Neck in the Middle Patuxent River; the Beech Grove circles to the left and down to the Little Patuxent River. Most hiking is along wide pathways, save for rocky and narrow stretches near the Middle Patuxent. The walks are surprisingly flat except for steep descents to the shoreline.

Not so flat is the short, yellow-blazed Pick Rock Loop, which charges down the hill to the river and back. A 1.5-mile white-blazed spur here leaves the I-95 bridge along a wooded ridge. If you choose, at the end of this out-and-back trail you can return on overgrown deer trails in the stream valley along the river.

Trail Sense: The trails are blazed and a there is a mapboard.

Dog Friendliness
Dogs are permitted on all the Savage Park trails.

Traffic
The park is generally lightly used.

Canine Swimming
There is ample opportunity for dog paddling at Savage Park, the best coming in the Middle Patuxent River where access is easiest.

Trail Time
More than an hour.

10
Soldiers Delight NEA

The Park
Soldiers Delight NEA's 1900 acres are part of a prairie-like grassland that rests on igneous rock that is one of only three such formations in North America. Early settlers called the area of Blackjack Pines and Post Oaks "The Barrens" because its low nutrient level was unfriendly to cultivation. The distinctive green rock was named "serpentine" for its resemblance to a snake native to northern Italy. This arid soil has produced a landscape more common in the American West than suburban Baltimore. Here you will find rare insects, rocks and at least 39 endangered plant species.

Baltimore County

Distance from the Beltway
- 8 miles from Exit 18
Phone Number
- (410) 922-3044
Website
- www.dnr.state.md.us/publiclands/central/soldiers.html
Admission Fee
- None
Directions
- Soldiers Delight is west of Owings Mills. From I-795 take Franklin Boulevard West to Church Road. Go right and left on Berrymans Lane and left on Deer Park Road to the Visitor Center on the right.

The Walks
The thing that makes Soldiers Delight so unique and visually appealing - the serpentine barrens - does not do hiking dogs any favors. The green-tinted stone is embedded in probably half of the park's seven miles of trails, jutting through the soil in hard ridges. So little soil accumulates in the barrens that the Maryland Geological Survey locates its seismic recording station here because such ready access to the bedrock makes it a simple matter to record vibrations during earthquakes. Soldiers Delight, so easy on the eye, can be tough on the paw.

The trail system is essentially two loops connected at the Deer Park Road Overlook. While the terrain rolls up and down there are

> **Bonus**
> The first chromium mines in America were opened here in 1808 and from 1828 to 1850 just about every scrap of chrome in the world came from Soldiers Delight. Along the Choate Mine Trail you can stand in front of the entrance to the Choate Mine and look into the slanting holes kept open by half-timbered posts. So close the cool air wafting up from the mine will rustle your dog's fur.

no tough climbs on these hikes. The woods are airy - and will become more so. The Virginia pines and Eastern Red Cedar you see are invasive species being removed by prescribed burning.

Trail Sense: The well-marked trails are shown own a trail map.

Dog Friendliness
Dogs are permitted throughout Soldiers Delight.

Traffic
The trails are for hikers and are seldom crowded.

Canine Swimming
Swimming is limited at Soldiers Delight; Red Run (on the Dolfield and Red Run Trails) and Chimney Branch (on the Serpentine Trail) are rarely knee-high to a dogleg.

Trail Time
More than an hour.

11
Loch Raven Reservoir

The Park

Robert Gilmor, son of a successful Baltimore merchant, bought 2,000 acres in the Gunpowder River valley with dreams of building a castle resembling those of his ancestral Scotland. His mansion Glen Ellen never quite accomplished his vision and the estate was sold to the city just before he died in 1883. A dam and water tunnel to funnel water into Baltimore were built in 1881 and enough property was acquired by the 1920s to raise the height of the dam and create the 10-mile long Loch Raven Reservoir - the name being a tip of the hat to Robert Gilmor's beloved Scottish lochs.

Baltimore County

Distance from the Beltway
- 2 miles from Exit 27
Phone Number
- (410) 795-6151
Website
- None
Admission Fee
- None

- Loch Raven Reservoir is accessed from Exit 27 of the Baltimore Beltway (I-695) on Dulaney Valley Road (MD 146). Some of the more popular parking areas can be found on Seminary Road, Providence Road, Morgan Mill Road at Loch Raven Road, the Dulaney Valley Road bridge, Warren Road and at the end of Pot Springs Road.

The Walks

There is enough hiking on wide fire roads at Loch Raven to require days to complete. Throw in the ubiquitous side trails and it could take a dog's life to see the entire watershed. All the trails through the buffer zone around the "loch" are heavily wooded with mature trees that help protect the reservoir's water quality. Many of the trails track along high ridges with commanding views of the water, especially when the trees are not in leaf.

> **Bonus**
> Simply having the opportunity to hike these scenic trails is the biggest bonus at Loch Raven. Most municipalities do not allow access to its reservoirs and in fact recreational use here is an on-going experiment. If any activity is judged to adversely affect the water supply (like dogwalking) for Loch Raven's 1.8 million users, the privilege will be withdrawn.

A day of hiking Loch Raven will involve many hill climbs, some that will leave both human and dog panting. There are stream crossings and rough stretches of trail, especially through ravines.

Trail Sense: Mapboards showing mountain biking routes are at some trailheads but for the most part you will be your own navigator. Orient yourself to the reservoir as you create hiking loops.

Dog Friendliness
Dogs are allowed on the trails throughout Loch Raven.

Traffic
Loch Raven is a hotbed for mountain bikers and you can encounter the occasional horse. Loch Raven Road is closed to traffic on the weekends from 10 a.m. to 5 p.m. to better accommodate recreational users. Trail use lessens north of Dulaney Valley Road.

Canine Swimming
Swimming and wading are not permitted in Loch Raven.

Trail Time
More than an hour.

12
Cromwell Valley Park

The Park
Cromwell Valley Park is the result of the melding of three former farm properties by Baltimore County in 1994. The land has been cultivated for nearly 300 years and a Christmas tree farm still operates here. Four iron mines once produced ore near the headwaters of Minebank Run and the valley evolved into a major producer of agricultural lime. The remains of kilns used to cook Cockeysville marble into lime powder are still visible in a hillside along the stream.

Baltimore County

Distance from the Beltway
- 1 mile from Exit 29
Phone Number
- (410) 887-2503
Website
- www.co.ba.md.us/p.cfm/agencies/recparks/cromwell.cfm
Admission Fee
- None
Directions
- Cromwell Valley Park is east of Towson on Cromwell Bridge Road (MD 567), north of Exit 29 of the Baltimore Beltway (I-695).

The Walks
Still a young park, Cromwell Valley has already become a favorite with Baltimore area dog walkers. The park's 367 acres begin in a mile-wide riparian stream valley and taper across open fields and pastures until reaching upland forests.

Six short marked trails, totalling about 4 miles, visit all corners of Cromwell Valley. Most of the walking is on wide former farm roads. For a flat, easy stroll walk the length of the out-and-back Minebank Run Trail for 1.2 miles. Although you are only yards from the stream the water is seldom seen but the shrubs and small trees that shelter the banks are a haven for songbirds. The Willow Grove Trail climbs steadily to the top of a ridge for a loop through woods filled with tall, straight yellow poplar trees.

> **Bonus**
> The sport of orienteering began as a military training exercise in Scandinavian forests in the last decades of the 19th century. It came to America in 1967 at Valley Forge, Pennsylvania. The term "orienteering" comes from the military practice of orientation, finding ones way through unfamiliar ground with a "chart and compass." Cromwell Valley has developed a permanent self-guided course for the practioners of the art. Pick up a topographical map in the office at Sherwood Farm and challenge your dog's nose in a wayfinding contest.

Trail Sense: A trail map is available at the parking lot. The trails are blazed but not always reliably so. This is generally not a concern except on the red-blazed Willow Grove Trail where a missed turn (easy to do) can land you on the Loch Raven trail system with its miles of uncharted hiking.

Dog Friendliness

Dogs are allowed throughout Cromwell Valley Park.

Traffic

Bikes and horses are not permitted on the park trails.

Canine Swimming

Minebank Run is a gurgling little flow of water that is good for cooling off on a hot day but little more.

Trail Time

More than an hour.

13
Piney Run Park

The Park
In 1975 Piney Run was dammed to provide drinking water for Sykesville. The resulting reservoir covers 298 acres and the surrounding park that grew up around the lake is another 200 acres.

The Walks
Piney Run Park features more than 5 miles of wooded lakeside trails. The marquee trail here is the 3.5-mile Inlet Trail but canine hikers may want to start explorations on the .7-mile Field Trail Loop, especially for early arrivers. Dogs are allowed on this trail off-leash and under voice control until 8:00 a.m. Despite its name, most of this trail is under groves of Norway Spruce, Scotch Pine and White Pine.

Carroll County
Distance from the Beltway
 - 14 miles from Exit 18
Phone Number
 - (410) 795-3274
Website
 - None
Admission Fee
 - $4 for Carroll County residents; $5 for non-residents
Directions
 - Piney Run Park is north of Sykesville. From Exit 76 of I-70 take MD 97 North. After 5 miles look for Obrecht Road and make a right. Go 1 mile and make a left on White Rock Road. After another mile make a right on Martz Road and follow to park at end. To reach the equestrian trails, stay on White Rock Road to Liberty Road (MD 26). Make a right and another right on Martz Road and go 1 mile to parking area.

The Field Trail also has the best access to the Piney Run shoreline of any of its four trails.

The Inlet Trail is essentially a long lasso of a trail with three scenic paths intersecting the loop. A surprising amount of this hike is on paw-friendly grass and the trails are uniformly wide and easy to walk. The Inlet Trail takes in both cultivated farm fields and a variety of forest habitats. Near the trailhead the Inlet Trail connects to the Indian Trail loop and then the Lake Trail, both wooded paths less than 1/2 mile long. The Lake Trail is a flat,

> **Bonus**
> Nailed to a post along the Indian Trail is a dugout canoe. No longer seaworthy, the wooden canoe is still an unexpected reminder of how transportation used to take place at Piney Run before dams and power boats.

semi-arc trail that features snatches of pretty lakeviews through the trees; the Indian Trail is a narrower pick-your-way hike in the deciduous forest.

Across the lake are nearly 4 miles of equestrian trails for hikers who prefer their trails a bit less groomed, but free of charge. The southern trail is a linear trail along the shoreline; the northern section features more loops. Again, these Piney Run trails are wooded.

Trail Sense: A trail map is available; signs indicate trailheads and wooden posts with inlaid painted circles mark the trails. If that isn't enough to keep you on course there are map signs scattered through the park.

Dog Friendliness

Dogs are permitted on the trails at Piney Run and you can picnic with the dog here as well.

Traffic

Bikes are allowed only on the Inlet Trail. Most of the people who pay to get in are more interested in the water activities than the hiking trails.

Canine Swimming

The trails seldom touch Piney Run Lake but when they do the dog paddling is excellent.

Trail Time

More than an hour.

14
Patuxent Research Refuge - North Tract

The Park
A scrawl of the pen by Franklin Roosevelt in 1936 established the Patuxent Research Refuge as America's only refuge to support wildlife research. The original 2,670 acres swelled to its current size of 12,750 acres with the addition of 8,100 acres formerly belonging to adjacent Fort Meade (visitors must sign a waiver regarding possible live ammunition encountered on the grounds - don't let your dog dig in strange holes!). It is said that the Patuxent Research Refuge is the largest patch of undeveloped green space that can be seen from the air on the east coast between Boston and Raleigh. There are two sections of the refuge open to the public: the National Wildlife in Prince Georges County and the North Tract.

Anne Arundel County
Distance from the Beltway
  - 11 miles from Exit 7
Phone Number
  - (301) 497-5580
Website
  - http://patuxent.fws.gov
Admission Fee
  - None
Directions
  - The North Tract can be reached from the Baltimore-Washington Parkway, exiting to the east on Savage Road (MD 32). Make a right on Fort Meade Road (MD198) and after .7 miles a left on Bald Eagle Drive (marked by refuge sign).

The Walks
There are some 20 miles of trails in the North Tract, including the paved 8-mile Wildlife Loop access road which is lightly traveled. Another 9 miles of trails are on former access roads closed to vehicular traffic. The hiking on these pebbly roads cuts through the woods and, while quiet and solitary, the scenery seldom changes on the long, straight stretches.

The best hiking at the North Tract is on the Forest Habitat Trail, opposite the visitor center. The wide, soft trail contours pleasantly as it circles for 2.5 miles through mature forest with limited

> **Bonus**
> The wide diversity of habitats at Patuxent support at least 40 on-going research studies. The most famous research done here was conducted on the pesticide DDT. Rachel Carson used the data in her influential book, Silent Spring, to argue that DDT weakened the shells of bird eggs, preventing them from supporting the hatchlings. The research led to the banning of DDT and launched the moder n environmental movement. Today more than 250 species - 8 of every 10 birds that can be seen in the Baltimore area - have been sighted at Patuxent, including a pair of nesting bald eagles in the North Tract.

understory. Two other hiker-only trails of less then a mile are available: the Little Patuxent River Trail which loops through the moist ground by the river and the sandy Pine Trail.

Trail Sense: A descriptive trail map is available and the trails are marked at junctions with colored metal emblems.

Dog Friendliness
Dogs are permitted on all trails in the refuge.

Traffic
Will be light wherever you hike. Bikes and horses are restricted to the road-trails.

Canine Swimming
Several alluring ponds await canine swimmers including Rieve's Pond off the Blue Trail and the Cattail Pond at Bailey's Bridge. The Little Patuxent River a few feet from the pond has a deep pool at this point as well.

Trail Time
More than an hour.

15
Hashawha Trails

The Park

Carroll County maintains nearly 8 acres of open space for every 100 residents and nearly 1900 of those acres are at the Union Mills Resorvoir Site. In 1972 the county purchased the land to establish the Bear Branch Nature Center and the surrounding Hashawha (an Indian term meaning "old fields") Environmental Center trails.

The Walks

There is something for every canine hiking taste at the well-designed Hashawha trails. Out for a simple trot? The blue blazed Vista Trail is a 1.2-mile circuit on mostly level ground that takes in fields, woods and ponds. Toss in the Stream Trail (green blazes) and you add a restored log cabin, grassy meadows, the gurgling Bear Branch Creek and a boardwalk crossing over part of Lake Hashawha. This blue-green circuit totals a bit less than 3 miles. For longer hikes take to the wooded hills of the Wilderness Trail (yellow blazes) where four loops pile upon one another until reaching Big Pipe Creek. The complete outer loop brings 2.2 miles of rolling and sometimes rocky trails into your hiking day. Looking for an all-day hiking adventure? There are 8 more miles of marked trails laid out by the Carroll County Equestrian Council, including the Kowomu Trail, beyond the Hashawha trails. These can also be accessed from their own parking lots; be aware that hunting restrictions close these trails from September

Carroll County

Distance from the Beltway
- 23 miles from Exit 19
Phone Number
- (410) 848-2517
Website
- ccgov.carr.org/hashawha
Admission Fee
- None
Directions
- Hashawha is north of Westminster. Go north on Route 97 and turn right on John Owings Road. Go 1.5 miles and make a left on Hashawha Road. The Nature Center is up the hill on the right.

> **Bonus**
> Here is the chance for your curious dog to look a bald eagle in the eye. The Nature Center maintains a M.A.S.H. unit for raptors who have been injured too badly to be returned to the wild. The cages for eagles, kestrels, hawks, owls, turkey vultues and other recovering birds of prey are on the Vista Trail.

through February on Mondays, Wednesdays and Fridays and for two weeks after Thanksgiving. Don't overlook the short interpretive Bear Path trail behind the Nature Center that helps explain our everyday environment.

Trail Sense: The trails are well-marked and trail maps and a mapboard are available at the Nature Center. Grab a map because there are many opportunities to slip mistakenly onto a crossing horse trail or adjoining private property.

Dog Friendliness
Dogs are permitted wherever you are allowed to hike.

Traffic
No horse or motorized vehicles are allowed on the Hashawha trails; the remote Union Mills Equestrian Trails may require yielding to the odd horse.

Canine Swimming
The streams at Hashawha provide a welcome splash on a hot day but aren't deep enough for extended dog paddling.

Trail Time
More than an hour.

"Any man who does not like dogs and want them does not deserve to be in the White House."
— *Calvin Coolidge*

16
Cylburn Arboretum

The Park
Jesse Tyson, heir to a family chrome fortune, began developing Cylburn estate in 1863 by starting construction on a gray stone Second Empire mansion. His home was not ready to live in until 1888 and Tyson, a lifelong bachelor then in his 60s, celebrated by taking a 19-year old wife, Edyth Johns. "I have the fairest wife, the fastest horses and the finest house in Maryland," boasted Tyson. When he died 16 years later his wife carried on the family matrimonial tradition by marrying a younger man. When she died in 1942, husband Bruce Cotton sold the property to the city of Baltimore for a pittance so that the land would be used as a park. After housing neglected children for several years, the Cylburn Arboretum opened to the public in 1958.

Baltimore City

Distance from the Beltway
- 5 miles from Exit 13

Phone Number
- (410) 396-0180

Website
- www.cylburnassociation.org/index.htm

Admission Fee
- None

Directions
- Cylburn Arboretum is in northwest Baltimore at 4915 Greenspring Lane.

The Walks
The 176 acres of Cylburn Arboretum's grounds are visited by five loop trails. These passageways are wide and paw-friendly soft dirt or cedar mulch but you will still want to stray off the paths to read the labels of the many ornamental trees. Most of the walking is easy going along the top of a wooded ridge although the Woodland trail does plunge down a hillside. Beware of the Witch-Hazel Trail which is rocky under paw as it lopes down the same hill. There are also several garden areas to explore off the trails. The feature trail at Cylburn, the Circle Trail, is enveloped by the relentless pounding of traffic on I-83 but it eventually fades

> **Bonus**
> The collection at Cylburn Arboretum features several Maryland Big Tree Champions including an Italian maple and a paperback maple. Two easy champions to see are on the lawn in the right front of the mansion: a castor aralia with large glossy leaves and an Amur maackia. Both trees are native to Asia and are resilient to pests. The maackia is a member of the pea family discovered by 19th century explorer Karlovich Maack along the Amur River between Siberia and China.

into white noise.

Trail Sense: A trail map and map of the grounds are available; large signs are posted at trail junctions.

Dog Friendliness
Unlike many nature centers, dogs are allowed at Cylburn Arboretum and even welcome - the water fountain features a fill bowl for dogs.

Traffic
Only foot traffic is allowed on the Wildflower Trails.

Canine Swimming
None.

Trail Time
More than an hour.

17
Gunpowder Falls State Park - Jerusalem Mill

The Park
Established as a grain mill in 1772, Jerusalem Mill operated until 1961. Restoration began in 1985 and has expanded to include the entire Village of Jerusalem with tenant houses, smith shops, and a general store. Since 1995, the Jerusalem Mill has housed the administrative headquarters for all of sprawling Gunpowder Falls State Park.

Balt/Harford Counties
Distance from the Beltway
 - 8 miles from Exit 32
Phone Number
 - (410) 557-7994
Website
 - http://www.dnr.state.md.uspubliclands/central gunpowder.html
Admission Fee
 - None
Directions
 - The park office is in Kingsville on Jerusalem Mill Road off US 1.

The Walks
There are many miles of hiking along the Little Gunpowder Falls on both sides of park headquarters here. Upstream from Jerusalem Mill the white-blazed Little Gunpowder Trail is a bouncing ramble through the woods. The return trip on the linear trail can loop into the hillsides on blue-blazed side trails like the Quarry Trail. *Caution*: This trail requires one crossing of the 4-lane US 1 and although the road is not heavily used at this point the southbound traffic does race downhill around a blind curve like a banked NASCAR track.

Downstream (cross the bridge by the Mill to pick up the trail) the route takes in more open fields as it leads to a loop around the Kingsville Athletic Fields. For a quick loop, stop at the Jericho Covered Bridge and return on the yellow-blazed horse trail.

Trail Sense: A trail map is available and the trails are well-marked.

> **Bonus**
> Downstream from Jerusalem Mill about 1/2 mile is Jericho Covered Bridge, one of only six remaining covered bridges in Maryland and the only one of its kind in Baltimore and Harford counties. Old folk wisdom held that these bridges were built to resemble a barn to entice a wary horse across water but the bridges are covered simply to protect the expensive wooden decks. The ford at this point across the Little Gunpowder Falls dates to Colonial times; the bridge was constructed in 1865.
> Builder Thomas F. Forsyth used three truss types in its construction: the simple Multiple King Post; the horizontal Queen Post extension; and the Burr Arch, patented in 1804 by Theodore Burr, for stability. Renovated in 1981, the Jericho Covered Bridge still carries trafic.

Dog Friendliness
Dogs are permitted up and down the trails at Jerusalem Mills.

Traffic
The easy walking around Jerusalem Mill attracts many casual hikers and dog walkers; deep into the trails there is greater solitude.

Canine Swimming
The trails stay true to the whims of the Little Gunpowder Falls with many access points to the water.

Trail Time
More than an hour.

"Money will buy a pretty good dog but it won't buy the wag of his tail."
- Josh Billings

18
Rocks State Park

The Park
The trails through dense forests along the Deer Creek are on the first Maryland lands purchased specifically to become a state park, back in 1951. The area was originally settled by the Susqehannock Indians who staged ceremonial gatherings at the massive 190-foot rock outcroppings known as the King and Queen Seat. Today Rocks State Park encompasses 900 acres of land in three separate parcels.

The Walks
Chrome Hill Road. The trails at the signature section of Rocks State Park all lead eventually to the top of King and Queen Seat. The views of the lush forestland from the top of the rock pile are spectacular but the outcroppings are unfenced and great care is required for dogs near the cliffs. These are challenging trails with severe climbs and narrow passages studded with rocks and exposed stumps in places. The White Trail is a sporty loop trail up and down and around the mountainous knob; it accounts for most of the four miles of trails at Chrome Hill Road. A low-lying Nature Trail loop is a short, pleasant walk opposite the Hills Grove Picnic Area on St. Clair Bridge Road.

Falling Branch. In this 67-acre sanctuary a path leads to the base of Kilgore Falls, Maryland's second-highest vertical waterfall. At the falls, trails cross the stream to the base and climb to the top of the 30-foot downspout.

Harford County
Distance from the Beltway
- 19 miles from Exit 31

Phone Number
- (410) 557-7994

Website
- www.dnr.state.md.us/publiclands/central/rocks.html

Admission Fee
- There is a $2 per person charge for use of the three picnic areas.

Directions
- The park office is in the Chrome Hill Road section, 8 miles northwest of Bel Air on Route 24.

> **Bonus**
> The chance to watch rock climbers tackle the namesake rock outcroppings of the King and Queen Seat which rule over the waters of the Deer Creek as they have for centuries. Some of the vertical faces with people - no dogs in harness - hanging off them soar as high as 94 feet. There are climbing routes for the novice and challenges for the expert, especially Superbulge on Breakway Wall.

Hidden Valley Natural Area. Quiet! That is what awaits you in this undeveloped tract of woods about five miles north of Rocks. Your one-mile stroll along level ground beside Deer Creek will end at an idyllic spot beneath a jagged rock crag protecting dark pines. While you drink in the serenity your dog will enjoy the spa-like rapids in the shallow stream.

Trail Sense: A trail map is available for Chrome Hill Road and the trails are well-marked with colored blazes. No map is needed in the other areas.

Dog Friendliness

Dogs are permitted on the trails in Rocks State Park. Dogs are not permitted in any of the three picnic areas.

Traffic

The postage stamp-sized parking lots capable of holding only a half-dozen or so cars are an immediate tip-off that your visit to Rocks will not involve a day of elbowing your way through the trails.

Canine Swimming

There is plenty of access to Deer Creek from the parking lots but not the trails. At Falling Branch you will find wonderful pockets of water ideal for a doggie dip.

Trail Time

More than an hour.

19
Truxtun Park

The Park

Truxtun Park remembers Thomas Truxtun, a privateer in the American Revolution who impressed George Washington enough to be brought into the new United States Navy. Truxtun, the 8th recipient of the Congressional Gold Medal, outfitted the *U.S.S. Constellation* and was the earliest known user of signal flags aboard ship in the American navy. Looking down on Spa Creek, Truxtun Park is the Maryland state capital's largest park, covering 70 acres.

Anne Arundel County

Distance from the Beltway
- 20 miles from Exit 4
Phone Number
- None
Website
- None
Admission Fee
- None
Directions
- The park is in Annapolis between Spa Road and Bay Ridge Avenue. The main entrance is on Primrose Road off Hilltop Lane.

The Walks

At Truxtun Park you'll be trading the sculptures, manicured grounds and forced walkways of nearby Quiet Waters Park for rusting hulks of abandoned autos and free-flowing, hard-packed dirt trails - which suits most dog owners just fine. The trails roll over two large wooded hills separated by a ravine. In the recreational part of the park the Annapolis Striders have constructed a crushed stone path with built-in steps to navigate the slopes and help arrest erosion. Natural trails, including one route on the ridge above Spa Creek, cross the more isolated back section of the park.

A more extended canine hiking opportunity here is the Spa Creek Trail. This 1.5-mile route leaves Truxtun on a wooden bridge through high reeds and heads towards Spa Creek Conservancy and on to the former Bates High School.

> **Bonus**
> What dog doesn't enjoy the action of a good up-and-down-the-court basketball game? Some of the best outdoor basketball courts in Maryland can be found at Truxtun Park, including permanent bleachers to stop and watch the games.

Trail Sense: There are no maps and no trail guides. Get out and explore this compact park.

Dog Friendliness
Dogs are permitted across Truxtun Park.

Traffic
Truxtun can be a busy recreational park but the crowds seldom spill out onto the trails.

Canine Swimming
In a few spots the trails dip down to the waterline of Spa Creek for deep water canine aquatics.

Trail Time
Less than an hour.

20
Morgan Run NEA

The Park
The land that would eventually be preserved as the Morgan Run Natural Environment Area was settled in the early 1700s when a stagecoach road (now Liberty Road) was established between Baltimore and Frederick. Carroll County leads Maryland in agricultural preservation and these 1400 acres of natural land are slated to grow to more than 3000 in the future.

The Walks
Step out of the car onto the gravel parking lot and this *looks* like a place to walk the dog. Wide grass trails cut into rolling fields dip and dart across the horizon into woodlands. There are many intersecting trails cut through the grass (sometimes high) to extend the canine hiking experience here. When the trails reach the wooded areas at the cold, clear waters of Morgan Run they continue to be a paw-friendly, hard-packed dirt.

There are unconnected trails on either side of Morgan Run in the floodplain. Although these are hiker-only trails they are narrow and can be overgrown; a special trip to try them is not recommended.

Trail Sense: The trails are unmarked; trails maps exist but not at the park. Keep your internal gyroscope tuned up if you come without map and compass.

Carroll County
Distance from the Beltway
 - 17 miles from Exit 18
Phone Number
 - None
Website
 - None
Admission Fee
 - None
Directions
 - Morgan Run NEA is south of Westminster, just off MD 97. After a left on Bartholow Road, turn left on Jim Bowers Road after .1 mile and another immediate left on Ben Rose Lane to the parking lot at the end in .6 mile. The hiking and angler trails are in the north section at the end of Jim Bowers Road off Nicodemus Road from MD 97.

> **Bonus**
> Hiking with the dog and the horse?
> Carroll County offers several equestrian trails
> but none with the feeling of vast open spaces
> like Morgan Run.

Dog Friendliness

Dogs are permitted on these trails; it seems a shame to come without one.

Traffic

These trails are popular with equestrians but not crowded. The routes along Morgan Run are hiker-only. Bikes are not allowed in this Designated Wildland Area either.

Canine Swimming

Morgan Run is a premier trout stream, especially in the winter. A modest 5 yards across in most places, it occasionally sports a canine swimming hole. A small pond can also sustain a doggie dip.

Trail Time

More than an hour.

21
Middle Patuxent Environmental Area

The Park

Charles Carroll, a devout Roman Catholic, left Ireland in 1688 to escape religious persecution and in 1702 acquired his first grant of 7,000 acres along the Middle Patuxent River. He would add another 3,000 acres and his son 50,000 more as the family grew to be the most powerful in Maryland. In the 1960s the Rouse Company deeded this property to Howard County when it was acquiring land to build nearby Columbia. Middle Patuxent Valley Association was organized in 1996 to protect 928 acres of diverse wildlife and vegetation in the Middle Patuxent Environmental Area, now managed by Howard County Parks and Recreation.

Howard County

Distance from the Beltway
- 17 miles from Exit 16

Phone Number
- (410) 313-4726

Website
- www.mpva.org/

Admission Fee
- None

Directions
- The park is located north of Clarksville. The entrance is on Trotter Road, east of Clarksville Road (MD 108).

The Walks

Although the going can get confusing at times, there are two basic hikes at Middle Patuxent. The main loop leading from the parking lot uses farm roads to reach the river and then circles back up to the crest of a ridge. Once you go down this trail you sign on for the entire loop which can take up to an hour. Often unmaintained, the hike can turn into a doggie steeplechase over fallen trees as the vegetation shifts from airy woodland to lush forest. Much of the trail is soft dirt but many areas are traversed on grass, a legacy of the Rouse days when the land was planted with ornamental non-native autumn olive trees and fescue grasses best suited for golf courses and lawns. If the grass has not been mowed it can be tough going. And watch for ticks!

> **Bonus**
> The mottled brown American Woodcock is a long-time favorite of birdwatchers who cherish its unique courtship display. In springtime, at dusk, males arrive at "singing grounds" and begin flying in upward spiraling circles before swooping back to earth where they herald their flights in song. Woodcocks require four habitats in close proximity: feeding cover, nesting cover, roosting areas and open ground for courtship. At Middle Patuxent seven acres have been set aside for woodcock habitat management.

The Southwind Trail has been created off the main loop and also leads to the river where majestic sycamore trees overhang the banks. The route travels up through Clegg's Meadow, decorated with warm-weather native grasses that have been reintroduced to the park.

Trail Sense: The Southwind Trail uses signposts but the main loop is sporadically marked. Consulting the map on the board in the parking lot is a must.

Dog Friendliness
Dogs are permitted on all the trails here.

Traffic
Foot traffic only is allowed at Middle Patuxent and it is light.

Canine Swimming
The banks of the Middle Patuxent River are often high but there is ample opportunity for a good swim.

Trail Time
More than an hour.

> *"Children are for people who can't have dogs."*
> *- Anonymous*

22
Eden Mill Nature Center

Harford County

Distance from the Beltway
 - 25 miles from Exit 31
Phone Number
 - (410) 836-3050
Website
 - www.edenmill.org
Admission Fee
 - None
Directions
 - Eden Mill Park is 7 miles west of Pylesville. The park is on Eden Mill Road off Fawn Grove Road between Route 136 (Harkins Road) and Route 165 (Federal Hill Road).

The Park

The first mill here was built in the early 1800s and named for Father Eden, a local priest. Save for a decade after World War I when the mill was converted into a power plant, flour, cornmeal and buckwheat were ground along Deer Creek almost continuously until 1964. At that point Harford County acquired the mill and surrounding 57 acres to settle the final owner's estate. The Eden Mill Nature Center was created in 1991 to preserve the mill and create the trail system through the property.

The Walks

There are 5 miles of trails at Eden Mill, including an elevated boardwalk, that stretch across 10 interconnecting paths. These trails are very easy on the paws - grass and soft dirt with only some rocky stretches on the incline of the High Meadow Trail. The Bluebird Trail is a special dog favorite with its grassy lanes through eye-high brush lending it the flavor of an English maze garden. The terrain at Eden Mill ranges from flat floodplain walking to hillside hiking that demand switchbacks to tackle the steep grades.

Trail Sense: A printed Trail Guide is available that allows you to create a hiking day of endless combinations of trails.

> **Bonus**
> On the Beaver Run Trail, along Deer Creek, a bench is built directly into the bank that is ideal for dangling your tired paws in the water as it moseys by.

Dog Friendliness
Dogs are permitted on the trails at Eden Mill.

Traffic
No bikes, cycles, motor vehicles or horses are allowed on the trails - just walkers on two legs or four.

Canine Swimming
There is good access to Deer Creek, which generally flows lazily along at canal speed.

Trail Time
More than an hour.

How To Pet A Dog
Tickling tummies slowly and gently works wonders. Never use a rubbing motion; this makes dogs bad-tempered. A gentle tickle with the tips of the fingers is all that is necessary to induce calm in a dog. I hate strangers who go up to dogs with their hands held to the dog's nose, usually palm towards themselves. How does the dog know that the hand doesn't hold something horrid? The palm should always be shown to the dog and go straight down to between the dog's front legs and tickle gently with a soothing voice to acompany the action. Very often the dog raises its back leg in a scratching movement, it gets so much pleasure from this.
-Barbara Woodhouse

23
Gunpowder Falls State Park - Pleasantville

The Park
This isolated trail system on the Little Gunpowder Falls comes to canine hikers courtesy of the Maryland and Pennsylvania Railroad, known affectionately as the Ma & Pa. To create the railbed nineteenth century railroad engineers clawed their way up the steep river valley here levelling hillsides and filling ravines. That railbed of the abandoned line now makes up the bulk of the hiking at Pleasantville.

The Walks
There are three hikes at Pleasantville, including a candidate for the "Least-Traveled Path" in the Baltimore area - the Pleasantville Loop. This 1.5-mile trek begins with one of the steepest climbs in the Gunpowder Falls State Park system to reach the start of the loop. Virtually indiscernible as a trail in most parts, let the dog lead the way and keep an eye out for white blazes. The loop follows a creative series of 270-degree turns through the forest with only occasional glimpses of the river below before returning to that steep stem trail.

The main hiking is across Pleasantville Road (a tricky crossing with a dog). Linear trails run along the river on both sides for two miles between Pleasantville and Bottom roads that can be combined for a loop across narrow bridges. The hike on the Baltimore County (white blazes) side is more topsy-turvy, tumbling in

Balt/Harford Counties
Distance from the Beltway
 - 9 miles from Exit 31
Phone Number
 - (410) 557-7994
Website
 - http://www.dnr.state.md.uspubliclands/central/gunpowder.html
Admission Fee
 - None
Directions
 - The Pleasantville section is southwest of Belair. From Harford Road (MD 147), take Fork Road west and make a right on either Bottom Road or, quickly following, Pleasantville Road. Parking is along the street and more plentiful at Bottom Road than Pleasantville.

> **Bonus**
> The Baltimore region offers many chances to hike along the right-of-ways of historic railroads, but perhaps none so exotic as here. It is easy to picture the slow-moving steam trains chugging through this lush valley as you amble along.

and out and around ravines; the Harford side (yellow blazes) uses more of the Ma & Pa trailbed, which crossed the river near the center of these trails, and is a bit tamer. It also adheres more closely to the flow of the river. The river is generally shallow enough to ford and shorten this 4-mile round trip.

Trail Sense: A trail map is available but not on site. The routes are always well-blazed in Gunpowder Falls State Park.

Dog Friendliness

Dogs are permitted on the trails at Pleasantville.

Traffic

These trails are so lightly used the lack of foot traffic can fail to keep the paths from getting overgrown.

Canine Swimming

Good, but there is not as much access to the river as might be expected due to high banks and vegetation.

Trail Time

More than an hour.

24
Double Rock Park

The Park

The land that now contains the 102-acre Double Rock Park was part of a 3,000-acre tract of land first surveyed in 1735 for English overseers William Chetwynd and John Whitwick. It is believed the new owners were interested in exploiting the virgin forests that blanketed the hills of the land they called Grindon. Served only by a very narrow gravel toll road known as the Baltimore and Harford Turnpike, settlement came slowly to the area. In 1874, city surveyor Simon Jonas Martinet purchased 35 acres of land about one mile west of present-day Double Rock Park which he named Parkville. On the heels of the suburban migration following World War II, the park was dedicated in 1947.

Baltimore County

Distance from the Beltway
 - 1 mile from Exit 31
Phone Number
 - None
Website
 - None
Admission Fee
 - None
Directions
 - From I-695 take Exit 31 South (Harford Road) to Parkville. After 1/4 mile cross Putty Hill Avenue at the top of a hill and go downhill for 1/2 mile to Texas Avenue. Turn left and go one mile to the end at Glen Road. Cross road into park entrance.

The Walks

A popular ball-playing and picnic park on the top of a hill, the active dog owner can find enchanting trails down below. The wide dirt paths are completely wooded with plenty of elevation changes throughout the trail system. The Yellow Trail, picked up to the right of the parking lot, works around the perimeter of the property and is joined at several junctions by the Red Trail which meanders down and around Stemmer's Run. The stream was restored in 1997 and has a number of interesting nooks and crannies as it flows through the park. The blue-blazed

Bonus
Save for the arboreal graffiti artist's assault on the many smooth-barked beeches on the hillsides, Double Rock ofers a good imitation of a rural wilderness area. The immersion into nature happens quickly with a descent from the parking lot that immediately leaves the neighborhood houses behind. For a residential area the trails are clean (although the stream is a magnet for cups and bottles and wrappers).

Falls Trail starts down the stairs from the parking lot and follows a macadam path two-tenths of a mile to a small waterfall.

The namesake rocks for Double Rock Park mark the entrance and are not worth a special trip; more intriguing are the rock perches on the hillside above the stream that make ideal rest stops for a tired dog.

Trail Sense: There is no trail map available and no mapboard at the park. The blazes on the trails are easy to follow however.

Dog Friendliness
Dogs are permitted throughout Double Rock Park.

Traffic
The shady picnic pavilions get the bulk of the visitation; cross the stream and enjoy the less-traveled trails.

Canine Swimming
Stemmer's Run is not deep enough for anything other than a refreshing splash.

Trail Time
More than an hour.

25

Prettyboy Reservoir

The Park

In 1775 William Hoffman, recently arrived from Frankfurt, Germany, hacked his way through the wilderness to the West Branch of Great Gunpowder Falls to build Maryland's first paper mill. Hoffman's Clipper Mill is said to have produced paper for Continental currency during the Revolution. The state's paper industry thrived here for a century before giant mills in the West usurped its business. The river was dammed in 1933 to create Prettyboy Reservoir for a thirsty Baltimore. The colorful name survives from a local farmer's favorite horse that perished in a nearby stream.

Baltimore County

Distance from the Beltway
- 24 miles from Exit 24
Phone Number
- None
Website
- None
Admission Fee
- None
Directions
- Prettyboy Reservoir is southwest of Middletown, west of Exit 31 off I-83. Middletown Road will lead to several roads with trailheads including Spooks Hill Road, Beckleysville Road and Gunpowder Road.

The Walks

Baltimore City controls 7,380 heavily timbered acres along 46 miles of shoreline in the Prettyboy watershed. Hiking is almost exclusively on fire roads and involves many long climbs and descents. Ignore the occasional footpath that radiates off the grass-and-dirt roads - invariably they will lead to a dead-end or become overgrown.

Most of the trekking is done high above the water level and the reservoir is only rarely glimpsed. Instead, it is the richness of differing forest types and not lake views that is the enduring beauty of Prettyboy. The reservoir slopes have been regularly logged and the forests are in differing stages of succession.

> **Bonus**
> The best hiking at Prettyboy is out of sight of the reservoir and along the Gunpowder Falls, accessed by pull-offs on Gunpowder Road. Here you'll find walks through dense hemlock forests, none more special than the hike back in time to Hemlock Gorge. For this one, leave the fire roads behind and walk down a narrow dirt path on the northeast side of the bridge over the river. After crossing a tumbling stream the towering hemlocks begin in earnest, blocking out all other plants except the mosses clinging to the rock outcroppings on the steep slopes. When the river bends 90 degrees to the right, it serves up one lasting impression of Hemlock Gorge before the trail fades away. Scarcely, a half-mile long there is a good amount of rock scrambling and log-hopping for a fairly robust dog to follow the river.

Trail Sense: Fire road trailheads are marked by orange barrier posts. Beyond that there is nothing. The emergency fire roads will eventually collide with a main road.

Dog Friendliness
Dogs are permitted on the trails in the Prettyboy watershed.

Traffic
It is almost an event of cosmic intervention to encounter a horse, mountain biker or fellow hiker on the trail during an outing at lightly used Prettyboy Reservoir.

Canine Swimming
There is some splashing and dog paddling available in Gunpowder Falls but there are long stretches without water here.

Trail Time
More than an hour.

26
Quiet Waters Park

The Park

Traces of human habitation dating back 5000 years have been found along Harness Creek. The water's name descends from Englishman William Harness who claimed a tract of land here in 1652. For the next three centuries the original land was divided and sold into various estates until 1976 when the entire property was deeded to Mary Parker by the Simplicity Land Company. In 1987 Anne Arundel County purchased 336 acres of woodland on the banks of the South River and Harness Creek to create Quiet Waters Park, which opened in 1990.

Anne Arundel County

Distance from the Beltway
 - 22 miles from Exit 4
Phone Number
 - (410) 222-1777
Website
 - http://web.aacpl.lib.md.us/rp/parks/QuietWaters/
Admission Fee
 - There is a $4 daily vehicle charge; closed on Tuesdays
Directions
 - The park is located in south Annapolis on Quiet Waters Park Drive off Forest Drive.

The Walks

The dominant trail at Quiet Waters is an eliptical multi-use path that circles the many cultural and recreational amenities of the park from end to end. The east side of the path traverses grassy fields and wetlands while the west side is a curving exploration of the woodlands. There are so many contours that even on a crowded day you can find a bit of solitude on the trail. Several loops lead off the main 4-mile trail to views of the water. The walking is fairly easy and level throughout.

You may be tempted to step away from the wheeled traffic on this bike path and head down narrow dirt paths that radiate off the asphalt but do so only with an explorer's heart. The unmarked trails in the woods may or may not lead back to the main trail and may take you right off park property. Some of these

> **Bonus**
> The natural beauty of elegant Quiet Waters Park is augmented by the outdoor sculptures that grace the grounds. Sculptures are chosen by jury from national and international artists working with a variety of material and installed on a rotating basis.

natural trails roll up and down hills overlooking Harness Creek.

Trail Sense: A park map is available and will be very handy for hiking off the bike path.

Dog Friendliness
Quiet Waters Park is home to Anne Arundel County's first off-leash dog park, covering an acre of the back of the park. There are two enclosures - a large romping area for active dogs and a smaller, shadier playground for smaller and older dogs.

Traffic
This is a popular and busy park.

Canine Swimming
Through the trees behind the dog park is a secluded stretch of South River beach just for swimming dogs. The waves are gentle enough to entice even the wariest dog into the water.

Trail Time
More than an hour.

27
Rockburn Branch Park

The Park

In pre-Revolutionary times the Patapsco River was deep enough to welcome ocean-going ships as far upriver as this point, known as Elkridge Landing. Tobacco grown in Anne Arundel County fields (Howard County was formed in 1851) was housed and shipped here. The river was silting steadily, however, and the port was gone by 1800. Only the name plates of Landing Road in the 390-acre Rockburn Branch Park hints at the area's rich maritime heritage.

> **Howard County**
> Distance from the Beltway
>   - 5 miles from Exit 10
> Phone Number
>   - (410) 313-4955
> Website
>   - www.co.ho.md.us/rprock.html
> Admission Fee
>   - None
> Directions
>   - There are two entrances to Rockburn Branch Park. The South area is on Montgomery Road off US Route 1 west and the North area is accessed from Landing Road off Montgomery Road.

The Walks

There is plenty of dogwalking to be had in both the North and South areas of Rockburn Branch. The South area features a 4.25-mile trail that slips through a wooded natural area. This amiable hike rolls up and down hills that represent the last gasp of the Piedmont plateau before it gives way to the coastal plain. Do not cross the power lines since the trails on the other side are part of Patapsco Valley State Park where dogs are not allowed.

The hiking in the North area is less formal, including lightly forested trails in and around the disc golf course. Also here is an open field walking loop and the former bridle paths of the Clover Hill plantation.

Trail Sense: A park map is posted on parking lot bulletin boards. The main trail is blazed in yellow and uses signposts at trail junctions.

> **Bonus**
> Howard County preservationists have established the Rockburn Heritage Center as a depository for historic county buildings to join Clover Hill, a brick and frame mansion from the late 18th century that stands in the park. Currently its only companion is the Aaron McKenzie Bank Barn, a Civil War-era log barn. A third historic remnant, a 300-year old settler's barn was burned by arsonists in 2001.

trail junctions, but the rest of the park is discovered only by hiking around it.

Dog Friendliness

Dogs are permitted on the trails but not in the sports or picnic areas.

Traffic

This is a busy recreational park with activity on 8 athletic fields and picnic areas that spill onto the trails. Rockburn Branch is also a favorite with mountain bikers heading to the popular state park trails.

Canine Swimming

Rockburn Branch is a scenic, meandering little stream but not deep enough for canine aquatics. No ponds are in the park.

Trail Time

More than an hour.

"If you pick up a starving dog and make him prosperous, he will not bite you; that is the principal difference between a dog and a man."
                                            - Mark Twain

28

Benjamin Banneker Historical Park

The Park

Molly Welsh, an English indentured servant, gained her freedom and began growing tobacco on this property around 1690. She soon bought two African slaves, freeing the one called "Banneky" and marrying him. Benjamin Banneker was the grandson of that union. He had gained a local reputation for mechanical and mathematical prowess when three Quaker brothers from Pennsylvania arrived in the 1770s to build a flour mill on the Patapsco River. The Ellicott brothers befriended Banneker and lent him books to fuel his isolated studies. In 1791 he left his one-room homestead for the only time in his life to help Andrew Ellicott survey the boundaries for the new capital city of Washington. Upon returning he published an annual almanac of his astronomical observations from 1792 to 1797. Thomas Jefferson lauded the self-taught farmer who is remembered as a pioneering African-American scientist. Baltimore County purchased Banneker's former property in 1985 to establish a museum and 142-acre park.

Baltimore County

Distance from Baltimore
- 3 miles from Exit 13
Phone Number
- (410) 887-1081
Website
-www.thefriendsofbanneker.org
Admission Fee
- None
Directions
- The park is just east of Ellicott City. The entrance is on Oella Avenue off Frederick Road (MD 144). Parking for the Trolley Trail is plentiful in a lot on Oella Aveue and at the western terminus of Edmundsen Avenue.

The Walks

A good amount of serious hiking lies behind an unpromising little mulched trail that leads into the woods behind the picnic area at the back of the musuem. The wood chip trail is a short loop through a forest thick with a spicebush understory. A wide trail then shoots off the back of the loop and rolls downhill into a

> **Bonus**
> Near the Ellicott City terminus of the #9 Trolley Line is a railroad cut through solid rock that enables the train to reach town. A wooden boardwalk traverses this shady canyon; above cars rattle across a rickety iron bridge.

stream valley and eventually leaves the park to join the #9 Trolley Historic Trail. Turn right and the paved path curves uphill towards a residential area thinly veiled by border woods. To the left the trail slides downhill, following the Coopers Branch until reaching an overlook of Ellicott City.

Trail Sense: No maps or trail markings are available. Ignore the tempting side trails off the Trolley Trail - they lead uphill to deadends in backyards. A rare exception is the short side path near the start of the boardwalk that leads to a rock canyon carved by the tumbling Coopers Branch.

Dog Friendliness
Dogs are welcome in the park and on the #9 Trolley Trail.

Traffic
The #9 Trolley Trail is popular with dog walkers; fewer dogs take advantage of the groomed dirt trail in Banneker Park.

Canine Swimming
Coopers Branch is good for a cool splash in rocky pools but not sustained canine aquatics.

Trail Time
More than an hour.

29
Lake Waterford Park

The Park

This land was part of two land grants by Lord Baltimore, Gambriells Purchase and Howard's Pasture. An estate was carved from the property and a mill built to grind grain. After the mill was torn down in 1900 the area became known as a hiding place for hoboes. Subsequently, Waterford Mill, named for the 18th century Elizabeth Water, was farmed, used to raise commercial goldfish and even tried as a resort. Today Lake Waterford Park consists of 108 acres around the centerpiece 12-acre lake stocked with trout, carp, crappie, bass, pickerel and bluegill.

Anne Arundel County

Distance from the Beltway
 - 6 miles from Exit 4
Phone Number
 - (410) 222-6248
Website
 - http://web.aacpl.lib.md.us/rp/parks/lwp/index.html
Admission Fee
 - None
Directions
 - The park is in Pasadena at the corner of Pasadena Road and Waterford Road (MD 648).

The Walks

Don't dismiss Lake Waterford as another multi-use recreational trail upon seeing the paved paths at the trailheads. Beyond the picnic pavilions are a cornucopia of short, interconnecting nature trails. These are paw-friendly paths of sandy dirt and pine straw and the hiking is easy - wooden bridges and steps have been built to smooth out the rough spots.

The Blue Trail offers the most scenic diversion of the seven colored trails as it traces the lakeshore. There are many unmarked side trails as well, many of which are narrow fisherman's paths leading to the water. The trails are all wooded.

Trail Sense: A trail map is available but there is little chance of having to call out the St. Bernards here. The trails are not blazed but signposts lead the way at junction points.

> **Bonus**
> Lake Waterford sponsors an Adopt A Duck program to help support its population of domestic ducks and geese which are much in evidence as you walk on the paved section of trail by Lake Waterford.

Dog Friendliness
Dogs are permitted throughout Lake Waterford Park.

Traffic
Lake Waterford is a busy recreation and picnic park but competition is less fierce on the trails.

Canine Swimming
There are many access points along the trails for the dog to slip into Lake Waterford.

Trail Time
Less than an hour.

30
Northern Central Railroad Trail

The Park

The Northern Central Railroad began carrying passengers in 1838 but the road was known mostly to farmers and coal miners until November 18, 1863 when Abraham Lincoln boarded a regular coach, sitting with other passengers, headed for Gettysburg to dedicate a new national cemetery (contrary to popular folklore he did not scribble out the Gettysburg Address on the back of an envelope on the train). Less than two years later the President's funeral train would travel the same route. Passenger service would continue until 1972 when Hurricane Agnes finished the fading line by washing out bridges and tearing up track. The state of Maryland took possession of the NCRR in 1980 and after removing 600 tons of trash opened the first segment of the rail-trail in 1984.

> **Baltimore County**
>
> Distance from the Beltway
> - 6 miles from Exit 26
> Phone Number
> - (410) 592-2897
> Website
> - www.dnr.state.md.us/greenways/ncrt_trail.html
> Admission Fee
> - None
> Directions
> - The trail begins in Ashland, north of Cockeysville. From York Road (MD 45) turn right on Ashland Road. Stay on Ashland as main road bears left on Paper Mill Road and continue to parking lot at end.

The Walks

The 19.7-mile Northern Central Railroad Trail is the prettiest of the Baltimore area rail trails. Much of the route is decorated by isolated forests and meadows, occasionally dropping in on rustic farm towns. The first half of the trail roughly parallels the Big Gunpowder Falls (the Gunpowder Falls State Park administers the trail). The trail is broken up by nine parking lots so canine hikers with a two-car system can reduce the trail to manageable 2-3 mile segments. The crushed stone and clay path follows a

> **Bonus**
> The Northern Central Railroad's legacy of 135 years of passenger service is one of the longest in the world. Traces of that heritage can be seen in iron mile markers, old raiload signals, and the historic train station at Monkton. Put in operation in 1898 as a Pennsylvania Railroad Company stop, there are now railroading artifacts on display in the station which serves as a rest stop for trail users.

gentle 1% grade to an imperceptible rise of 400 feet from south to north.

Trail Sense: Trail maps are available and posted in the parking areas. Wooden markers signal trail distances.

Dog Friendliness

Dogs are permitted on the Northern Central rail trail.

Traffic

There are plenty of bikes and pedestrians and even the occasional horse along the trail.

Canine Swimming

Opportunities for a a quick doggie dip are easier to come by along the southern stretches, and so is drinking water.

Trail Time

More than an hour.

> *"We are alone, absolutely alone on this chance planet; and, amid all the forms of life that surround us, not one, excepting the dog, has made an alliance with us."*
> *- Maurice Maeterlinck*

31

Fort Howard Park

The Park

The British selected North Point, now part of Fort Howard Park and the southernmost point in Baltimore County, as the landing site for a 6-ship invasion force on September 12, 1814. In the pre-dawn hours 4700 British marines disembarked here to begin a 17-mile march on Baltimore. Later that day the Americans engaged the force in the Battle of North Point, slowing the invaders and triggering a demoralizing chain of events for the British that hastened the end of the War of 1812. The army returned to North Point in 1899 to build Fort Howard as the headquarters for the coastal defense of Baltimore. The fort was named for John Edgar Howard of the Maryland Continental Army who received one of only 14 medals awarded during the American Revolution for heroism at the Battle of Cowpens. In subsequent years the fort was an infantry training center (under General Douglas MacArthur for a time) through the Vietnam War, when a mock Vietnamese village was constructed here. The base was turned over to Baltimore County for use as a park in 1973.

Baltimore County

Distance from the Beltway
 - 4 miles from Exit 42
Phone Number
 - (410) 887-7529
Website
 - None
Admission Fee
 - None
Directions
 - Follow North Point Road through Fort Howard to its end at the VA Hospital and make a left into the park.

The Walks

The Endicott Trail is a paved walk through the "Bulldog at Baltimore's Gate" that enables your dog to ramble through the gun batteries and ammunition magazines and to clamber on top of the earth-covered parapets that are camoflauged from the open water. Although a dummy grenade was found in the picnic

> **Bonus**
> Where else can your dog climb into an actual battery and scan the Patapsco River just like gunnery officers who once aimed guns over the water capable of accurately firing 1,000 pound projectiles eight miles?

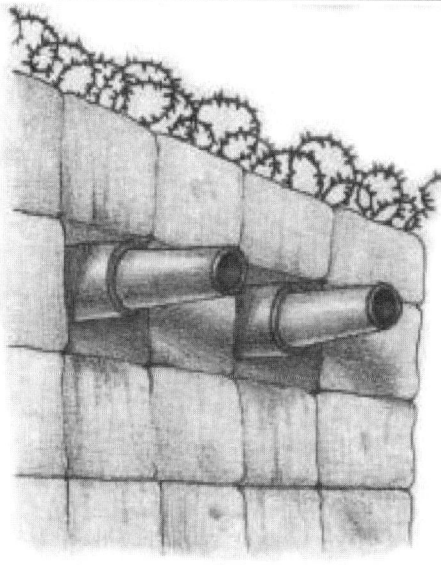

area in 1988 it is unlikely your dog will sniff out any old ordnance here. A nature trail - bushwhacking may be required - leads to the marshy extremities of the shady 61-acre park. Another trail follows under a Ropes Course 20 feet up in the trees. Keep four feet on the ground here.

Trail Sense: There is a faded mapboard in the parking lot that will make more sense after you explore the park on your own.

Dog Friendliness
Dogs are permitted throughout Fort Howard Park.

Traffic
Fort Howard Park ambles on in comfortable anonymity under the nose of its more illustrious neighbor up the peninsula, North Point State Park.

Canine Swimming
The shoreline is mostly broken seawall but there is access to the open water at a small stone beach - beware of broken glass and shells on paws.

Trail Time
Less than an hour.

32

Leakin Park/ Gwynns Falls Park

The Park

In 1922 J. Wilson Leakin, an attorney of means, died and gave Baltimore money from his rental properties to buy a large city park. Planners settled on the Gwynns Falls valley in western Baltimore, once the boundary of the Iroquoian and Algonquian speaking tribes. Much of the original land for the park when it opened in 1948 came from the estate of Thomas Winens which overlooked the Dead Run valley. Today Leakin Park and the adjoining Gwynns Falls Park, at 686 acres the largest public park in Baltimore, comprise over 1000 acres of recreational opportunity.

Baltimore City

Distance from the Beltway
 - 2 miles from Exit 17
Phone Number
 - (410) 557-7994
Website
 - None
Admission Fee
 - None
Directions
 - The entrance to Leakin Park is on Windsor Mill Road; a centralized parking location for both parks and the Gwynns Falls Trail is at the Winans Meadow Trailhead on Franklintown Road.

The Walks

Gwynns Falls is largely undeveloped so most of your hiking will be in Leakin Park. The trails are surprisingly lush for an urban park, with a thick understory thriving beneath towering trees. The primeval feeling of the park is so pervasive it was chosen as a filming site for the horror film *Book of Shadows: Blair Witch 2*.

Hiking on the spider web of trails at Leakin Park can be rough going. Expect rocky surfaces under paw, overgrown trails at points, and hearty hill climbs (one trail descends 50 steps and doesn't even go halfway down the hill). Your reward is near complete immersion in nature just minutes from the bustle of America's 13th largest city. Remnants of the Winans estate are sprinkled throughout the park: the family home, an 1850s stone Victorian mansion called Crimea; a wedding chapel; a water wheel;

> **Bonus**
> Thomas Winans made his fortune building the Russian transcontinental railroad for Czar Nicholas I. He learned railroading from his father Ross who invented the swivel wheel truck that enabled trains to negotiate curves. Their railroad heritage is preserved at Leakin Park by the Chesapeake & Allegheny Live Steamers who maintain 3 miles of track for miniature steam trains that carry passengers (sorry, no dogs) free of charge the second Sunday of every month. Capable of speeds of 25 mph, the trains rumble along at 6 mph.

and ruins of a mock fort that may have been built during the Civil War to deter Union troops from attacking the Winans, who sided with the Confederate rebels.

The first 4.5 miles of a planned 14-mile trail to the Inner Harbor, Gwynns Falls Trail, has been completed to Leon Day Park. The highlight of the trail, which is part paved and part rocky dirt, is on the east side of Gwynns Falls where it uses the Mill Race Path, a filled-in mill race where Baltimoreans once strolled in the early part of the 20th century. The mill race remained level while Gwynns Falls dropped as far as 80 feet below.

Trail Sense: A color trail map is available and you will be consulting it constantly as you travel these trails which aren't blazed. Signs show the way along Gwynns Falls Trail.

Dog Friendliness

Dogs are permitted throughout Leakin/Gwynns Falls Park.

Traffic

These are very lightly used trails.

Canine Swimming

Dead Run is an aptly named trickle of a stream and access to the swift-flowing Gwynns Falls is limited.

Trail Time

More than an hour.

33
Liberty Reservoir

The Park

When Liberty Dam walled off the North Branch Patapsco River in 1953 a reservoir greater in size than Loch Raven and Prettyboy combined gurgled into being. Its 9200 slender acres contain 82 miles of shoreline. There are many miles of attractive, isolated hiking on fire roads in the Liberty watershed but access along busy roads can be problematic for dog owners. Also, skitterish dogs would do well to avoid Liberty Dam Road where you'll find the closest thing to a park on the reservoir. The police shooting range and a local gun club are located here.

Balt/Carroll Counties

Distance from the Beltway
 - 8 miles from Exit 18
Phone Number
 - None
Website
 - None
Admission Fee
 - None
Directions
 - Liberty Reservoir is accessed primarily be three east-west roads that dissect the property: from north to south they are Westminster Road (MD 140), Deer Park Road, and Liberty Road (MD 26).

The Walks

The land in this valley before the plugging of the river was mostly pasture and cropland. Thus the wooded buffers around the reservoir are still filling in, giving these walks an airier feel than their water-holding cousins. But like Loch Raven and Prettyboy there is plenty of up-and-down hiking and the fire roads tend to make for long and straight routes.

There are several small creeks coursing through the watershed and trail crossings at these sites will be a wet shoe affair. Although not wide, officials have removed rocks from the stream bed to aide emergency vehicles in getting across. Good for trucks and dogs but not for hikers in cold weather.

Trail Sense: There is nothing. Come to Liberty with either a

> **Bonus**
> Pack your fishing rod with your hiking gear when you come to Liberty Reservoir, which has emerged as the home of Maryland's largest landlocked rockfish. Only a few years back the state record fish weighed 36 pounds but stripers of 40 pounds and more are being pulled regularly from the 3,100-acre lake. Liberty's unique water density and a high oil content that surrounds the egg sac of Chesapeake Bay strain rockfish allow for what biologists once thought impossible - the actual reproduction of rockfish in a small reservoir. Toss in regular meals of stocked trout and - voila! - giant fish.

map drawn by someone who has hiked these trails or a very flexible schedule. The fire road trailheads are identified by orange barrier posts.

Dog Friendliness
Dogs are permitted in the Liberty Reservoir watershed.

Traffic
Some Liberty trails are open to bikes and horses but all trails are lightly used.

Canine Swimming
The tributary streams feeding into the reservoir are better for splashing than swimming.

Trail Time
More than an hour.

> *"My dog can bark like a Congressman,*
> *fetch like an aide, beg like a press secretary*
> *and play dead like a receptionist."*
> — Gerald Solomon

34
North Point State Park

The Park

When European settlers began cultivating the wetlands and fields here in the 1640s, they were the latest arrivals in a string of human inhabitants stretching back 9000 years. Notoriety came to the North Point area during the War of 1812 when local Free Staters engaged British invaders. Happier times arrived a century later with the establishment of a small amusement park known as Bay Shore Park. Bethlehem Steel purchased the land in the 1940s and tore down the park to establish a private hunting preserve for its executives. The public was invited back in 1989 after the State of Maryland acquired the property for conversion into a 1310-acre park with more than 6 miles of shoreline along the Chesapeake Bay, Back River and Shallow Creek.

Baltimore County

Distance from the Beltway
 - 4 miles from Exit 42
Phone Number
 - (410) 329-0757
Website
 - www.dnr.state.md.us/publiclands/central/northpoint.html
Admission Fee
 - $2.00
Directions
 - North Point is east of Edgemere. From I-695 east of Baltimore, take Exit 40 to Route 151 south; from the west, use Exit 43. Follow signs to Fort Howard on North Point Road (Rt. 20). The park entrance is on the left, 1/2 mile from Miller Island Road.

The Walks

More than half the park consists of the Black Marsh Wildlands, considered to be one of the finest examples of a tidal marsh on the Upper Chesapeake. Unfortunately your dog will not see this unique landscape - dogs are not permitted in the Wildlands.

You can hike around the short Wetlands Trail Loop which is a hard-packed dirt path. Also available is a hike/bike trail that skirts some of the fields at the park. The stone surface is not

> **Bonus**
> Although only 20 acres in size, the Bay Shore Park was considered one of the finest amusement parks ever built along the Chesapeake Bay. Opened in 1906, the park featured an Edwardian-style dance hall, bowling alley and restaurant set in among gardens and curving pathways. There were rides such as a water toboggan and Sea Swing. Visitors would travel to the shore from Baltimore on a trolley line. Most of the park was torn down after its closure in 1947 but you and the dog can explore the remains of a turn-of-the century amusement park including the wood-framed trolley station and the restored ornamental fountain. Complete your tour with a hike down the old Bayshore Pier that juts almost a quarter-mile into the wind-swept Bay - a diving board once operated where benches rest today.

paw-friendly but does have wide grass shoulders. The old trolley line has been paved over in spots to form a nature trail. All the walking at North Point is flat and easy.

Trail Sense: A park map is available which indicates where trails are located.

Dog Friendliness

The opposite of most Maryland state parks, dogs are excluded from the wilderness areas and allowed in the developed parts of the park.

Traffic

Visitation is light enough to include the mile-long entrance road in your hiking agenda.

Canine Swimming

A small wading beach at the Visitors Center was opened in 1999 and dogs are welcome to dive in.

Trail Time

More than an hour.

35

The BWI Trail

The Park

The BWI Airport is the only commercial airport in the United States to offer visitors a recreational hiker/biker trail. Portions of the trail, most of which sit on airport property, have been opening since 1994. The 12.5-mile trail encircles the airport and is patrolled by Anne Arundel County.

The Walks

This is quite likely the noisiest dog walk you will ever take - airplanes, car traffic, trains. But after awhile it all fades into white noise and becomes part of the experience of this unique trail. That said, there are pastoral refuges along the route including woodlands, pine groves and even a horse farm.

For canine hikers the BWI Trail has several advantages over its rail-to-trail neighbors. Since it isn't constrained by a right-of-way, there is more grassy room on the shoulders for relief from the pounding of paw on asphalt (the trail is paved the entire way save for wooden boardwalks through wetlands); the trail was designed in a pleasing serpentine fashion; and there is a nice sprinkling of hills along the way. And, although few canine hikers are likely to care, the trail is a complete loop rather than an out-and back.

No matter how you plan to use the BWI Trail, take along drinking water for your dog as it is scarce along the path.

Trail Sense: A trail map is available but not on site (use the

---

Anne Arundel County

Distance from the Beltway
  - 4 miles from Exit 4
Phone Number
  - (410) 222-6244
Website
  - http:/www.dnr.state.md.us/greenways/bwi_trail.html
Admission Fee
  - None
Directions
  - The BWI Trail is west of Glen Burnie and south of Linthicum. Trail access and parking can be found on Andover Road on the north side of the trail and Dorsey Road (MD 176) on the south.

> **Bonus**
> The planes of course. The Thomas A. Dixon Jr. Aircraft Observation Area provides an ideal spot to watch the planes land directly in front of you. You won't be able to see the rubber hit the ground here but you can see it from other spots along the trail.
> To get the feel of a big jet soaring directly over your head, walk down a half-mile to the east (you'll see stop signs) and stand here. It won't be only jets using the airport either - you can spot an occasional propeller plane as well.

Internet or local park offices sometimes have one). While you can't get lost, the map does give mileage between landmarks to help plan your hiking day.

Dog Friendliness
Dogs are permitted all along the trail.

Traffic
Although less crowded than the nearby Baltimore & Annapolis Trail, to which the BWI Trail connects, there are still plenty of fast-moving humans in both directions to look out for.

Canine Swimming
None.

Trail Time
More than an hour.

36
Pine Valley Nature Center

Carroll County

Distance from the Beltway
 - 25 miles from Exit 19
Phone Number
 - None
Website
 - members.fortunecity.com/pinevalleynaturecenter
Admission Fee
 - None
Directions
 - Pine Valley Nature Center is in the north section of Manchester. From Main Street (Route 30) make a right onto York Street. Go 1/2 mile and turn left on Wilhelm Lane to the park.

The Park
The Pine Valley Nature Center was created in 1995 as an outdoor study area through a unique partnership between Manchester Elementary School and the town council. The school children voted to name their outdoor classroom Charlotte's Quest for the Outside World in honor of Charlotte Collett, a teacher and Council member who shepherded the project to reality.

The Walks
The 4 1/2 miles of trails at Pine Valley Nature Center are the most paw-friendly in the Baltimore area. You may want to shed your shoes and join your dog in hiking the soft grass trails barefooted. Even the dirt trails in the woods are often blanketed in spruce needles.

The trail system consists of nine short paths and visits an appealing mix of riparian meadows and woodlands. Trails lead to such attractions as Turk's Spring, the Stream of Life and Avian Cove. A Nature Trail winds around a wooded hillside. Like the trail surface, all the climbs at Pine Valley are gentle.

For a great game of fetch there is a large grassy field next to the Nature Center.

Trail Sense: The trails are not blazed but small concrete posts mark trail junctions. These posts are painted with a symbol indicating the trail but the pictures are sometimes worn away. A mapboard by the Nature Center sorts it all out but you will

> **Bonus**
> Take a moment to stop by the nature center's butterfly garden, a combination of annuals, perennials, trees, and woody shrubs that provide the proper environment for all stages of the butterfly's life cycle. You'll be bound to see some of nature's 28,000 species but don't expect them to be flying without warm sunshine - a butterfly can't take wing until its body temperature is 86 degrees.

likely not get lost in the park's compact 60 acres.

Dog Friendliness
Dogs are permitted on the trails at Pine Valley.

Traffic
The trails are for hikers and are seldom crowded when education programs are not scheduled. If the main gate is closed, you are welcome to walk into the Nature Center.

Canine Swimming
Walnut Pond is a quiet fishing hole that is an ideal spot for a doggie dip.

Trail Time
More than an hour.

37
Kinder Farm Park

The Park

In 1898 German immigrant A. Gustavus Kinder purchased 41 acres of farmland north of the Severn River and began growing fruits and vegetables for sale in Baltimore. The Kinders gradually expanded their agricultural operation until over 1,000 acres were under cultivation. After World War II, the Kinders moved from truck farming to cattle production and began selling off land for residential development. In 1979 they sold 288 acres of pastureland to Anne Arundel County for development as Kinder Farm Park.

> **Anne Arundel County**
>
> Distance from the Beltway
> - 7 miles from Exit 4
> Phone Number
> - (410) 222-6115
> Website
> - http://web.aacpl.lib.md.us/rp/parks/Kinder/
> Admission Fee
> - None; Closed Tuesdays
> Directions
> - The park is in Millersville, just west of Governor Ritchie Highway (MD 2) on Jumpers Hole Road.

The Walks

A 2.4-mile asphalt trail snakes around the Kinder Farm property visiting fields and meadows and dipping into reforestation areas. This is easy walking and connects to the East-West Boulevard Trail for even longer excursions.

More interesting to the canine hiker are the unimproved farm roads that run through the park. These sand/dirt paths duck into woodlands and across old fields. For the dog who has never been to a farm, a trail leads past the farmhouse/park office (circa 1926) and a close-up view of four concrete silos.

Trail Sense: None of the trails are marked at Kinder Farm Park but a park map is available.

> **Bonus**
> Back beside the secluded Bunk's Pond is a forest of bamboo, planted as an ornamental grass. Although mostly associated with southeast Asia, native bamboo is estimated to have once covered 5 million acres of the southeastern United States. Many of the 1200 species of this hardy grass grow eagerly in temperate regions like these timber bamboo plants that have sprouted to over 25 feet tall. They are wonderful at absorbing sound and make this pondside walk a quiet, special place. Beware under paw, however, as the trail has been cut through the stalks.

Dog Friendliness
Dogs are permitted throughout Kinder Farm Park.

Traffic
The paved perimeter trail sees the most use; horses are permitted on the natural trails.

Canine Swimming
There are four small ponds at Kinder Farm but because of aquatic vegetation or limited access these are not prime doggie swimming holes.

Trail Time
More than an hour.

> *"Ever consider what they must think of us? I mean, here we come back from the grocery store with the most amazing haul - chicken, pork, half a cow...They must think we're the greatest hunters on earth!"*
> *- Anne Tyler*

38
Gillis Falls Reservoir Site

The Park
Carroll County owns 1200 acres of land around the Middle Run and Gillis Falls where they are waiting approval to create a reservoir. In the meantime an equestrian trail system has been developed through the watershed by volunteers. These trails are closed Mondays, Wednesdays, Fridays and Saturdays from September 1 through February 28 and for two weeks beginning the Saturday after Thanksgiving due to a controlled hunting program.

Carroll County
Distance from the Beltway
- 21 miles from Exit 16
Phone Number
- None
Website
- None
Admission Fee
- None
Directions
- The Gillis Falls equestrian trails are east of Mt. Airy. From I-70 take Woodbine Road (MD 94) north off Exit 73. Make a left in about 1 mile on Newport Road, following signs to Carroll County Equestrian Center on Grimville Road.

The Walks
The Gillis Falls equestrian trails cover about 3.5 miles of wooded access roads. The terrain drops sharply in and out of the Gillis Falls stream valley on paths that feature many rocky stretches under paw. The elevation changes and varying moisture content of the soil conspire to allow differing forest types to dominate on different points of the hike. The trails are laid out in varying loops of short duration.

Hiking at Gillis Falls will necessitate at least two stream crossings and several more depending on your route. Only one bridge spans the sparkling clear stream waters. This is not a problem except at the confluence of Gillis Falls and Middle Branch which can be forded only by horse, dog or wet shoe.

Trail Sense: Trail maps are available but not at the trailhead. If you do not have a map, walk around the grass field in front of the parking lot and dip into the woods at obvious trail openings

> **Bonus**
> Civilization once took hold in the Gillis Falls valley and nature is slowly reclaiming building foundations, collapsed ruins and lampposts along the trail. One such cinderblock structure, now riddled with bullet holes, looks like a fomer hideout for Bonnie and Clyde.

and begin exploring. Yellow and black-striped ribbons are unreliably placed on trees.

Dog Friendliness
Dogs are permitted on the Gillis Falls equestrian trails.

Traffic
Be on the lookout for an occasional horse on a cross-country outing but there is little competition for these trails.

Canine Swimming
Stream waters are seldom deep enough for canine aquatics beyond splashing.

Trail Time
More than an hour.

39
Baltimore & Annapolis Trail

The Park
When the first steam train chugged out of Annapolis on the original Annapolis & Baltimore Short Line railroad in 1887 the track traversed woodlands and farm fields. The railroad quickly spawned towns along its route and at its peak 1.75 million people climbed aboard its passenger trains each year. When service was discontinued in 1968 the pattern of development was firmly entrenched. Today, one of every three dogs in Anne Arundel County lives within one mile of the Baltimore & Annapolis Trail Park. Since opening in 1985, the B&A Trail has been a model in the rails-to-trails movement, hosting an estimated one million users per year. The B&A is the 7th most heavily used rail-trail of more than 1000 such hikes across America.

Anne Arundel County

Distance from the Beltway
- 3 miles from Exit 4
Phone Number
- (410) 222-6244
Website
- www.dnr.state.md.us/greenways/b&a_trail.html
Admission Fee
- None
Directions
- The 13.3-mile linear park stretches from Glen Burnie in the north to Annapolis at the southern terminus. Park headquarters are located at the 7.0 mile marker where the trail crosses Earleigh Heights Road.

The Walks
The old rails have been converted into an asphalt ribbon ten feet wide, often with a grassy shoulder to step away from traffic. Dog walkers will be dodging joggers, cyclists, rollerbladers, strollers, equestrians and anything else man can dream of to put on wheels. Despite its heavy use, the B&A Trail is meticulously maintained by over 400 volunteer caretakers. More than 70 flowerbeds are strung like jewels along the route, which never exceeds a 1% grade.

> **Bonus**
> Near the 10-mile mark the B&A Trail crosses over Marley Creek where once stood a 140-foot railroad bridge that was washed away during Hurricane Agnes in 1972. Trail planners unearthed an historic highway bridge in Missouri to breech the creek but as it was being lifted into place on the trail in 1989, it crumbled. The present bridge is a hastily-built replacement.

The linear trail is most heavily used near the center at park headquarters, housed in a refurbished Victorian train station. The southern end of the trail, below College Parkway, is more rural and less crowded.

Trail Sense: A trail map and guide to historical markers are both available; mileage markers are placed every half-mile to help plan your turn-around location.

Dog Friendliness
Dogs are allowed at all points on the B&A Trail.

Traffic
Heavy, as noted.

Canine Swimming
None.

Trail Time
More than an hour.

> *"Dog. A kind of additional or subsidiary Diety designed to catch the overflow and surplus of the world's worship."*
> *- Ambrose Bierce*

40
Centennial Park

The Park
Within two years of opening in 1987 Centennial Park received the Merit Award for Innovative Design from the American Society of Landscape Architects. The centerpiece lake was created as a flood control measure in 1965 and now occupies 50 of the park's surrounding 325 acres.

The Walks
The park features over four miles of asphalt multi-use paths, most of which are featured on the 2.4-mile Centennial Lake trail around the water. This is a rolling, contoured exploration that keeps the lake in sight almost the entire way. The trail is mostly open on the south side and mostly shaded on the north where you will find the Howard County Arboreta, one of the best places to hike with the dog for an arboreal education. Many of the trees along the trail are marked for identification and most of Centennial Park's 60 or so species can be spotted from the path.

Trail Sense: Park maps can be studied on boards at the parking lot.

Dog Friendliness
Dogs are permitted everywhere in the park except on the athletic fields and in the picnic areas.

Howard County

Distance from the Beltway
- 13 miles from Exit 16
Phone Number
- (410) 313-7268
Website
- www.co.ho.nd.us/rpcent.html
Admission
- None
Directions
- The main park entrance is on Clarksville Pike (MD 108), north of Columbia. The West Area entrance is on Centennial Lane and the North Area entrance is on Old Annapolis Road.

> **Bonus**
> Columbia sprung into existence in the 1960s from the mind of James Rouse, an Eastern Shore shopping mall developer, as America's first planned city. Central to the plans were 80 miles of bikepaths connecting nine diverse villages, including three other man-made lakes near Centennial Park. Wilde Lake, where Columbia's first residents arrived in 1967, is a 1.5-mile cicumnavigation. If it feels as if you are walking the dog through someone's backyard at times, you are. Public access is reserved at some private lakeside properties. Trails also run alongside slender Lake Kittamaqundi at the edge of Columbia Town Center and two miles of paths surround 37-acre Lake Elkhorn.

Traffic
Centennial Park is a busy place and you'll be competing for space on the track with bikes, joggers, strollers, skaters and whatever else that moves.

Canine Swimming
On the north side of the lake there are a couple of places for the dog to slip into the water but that is all.

Trail Time
More than an hour.

41
Schooley Mill Park

The Park
Schooley Mill is a multi-use star in the Howard County park system. Much of its 192 acres is given over to equestrian activities and recreational pursuits.

The Walks
The simple trail system at Schooley Mill circles the perimeter of the property in two concentric loops. The outer loop is a mulch and dirt path through woodlands and wetlands; the inner loop uses old "carriage" roads, often on grass. There are 2 miles of wooded trails and 2 1/2 miles of roads through open meadows.

Howard County

Distance from the Beltway
   - 21 miles from Exit 16
Phone Number
   - (410) 313-6130
Website
   - www.co.ho.md.us/
     rpschool.html
Admission Fee
   - None
Directions
   - The park is southeast of Highland on Hall Shop Road between Clarksville Pike (MD 108) to the west and Skaggsville Road (MD 216) to the east.

Much of the hiking is easy going as the outer trail leads downhill to a stream valley where tulip poplars tower in the bottomlands. It follows the gurgling stream for a good distance and visits a secluded beaver pond. The trail system leads off-park for additional hiking in several places.

Trail Sense: A park map is available but the trails are not blazed. A more detailed map that indicates trail closings can be consulted on park bulletin boards.

Dog Friendliness
Dogs are permitted on the trails in Schooley Mill Park but not in the picnic or sports areas.

> **Bonus**
> On a hilltop in the center of the park is the James Marlow House. Built around 1840 as a two-story home with one room on each floor, it stands as an historic example of the agrarian vernacular architecture that once permeated Howard County. The log and chink exterior walls were covered with clapboard when the house was later enlarged.

Traffic
More people take advantage of Schooley Mill's playing fields, playgrounds and picnic areas than the hiking trails.

Canine Swimming
The beaver pond, which is packed into tight quarters, lures swimming dogs.

Trail Time
More than an hour.

"My dog is worried about the economy because Alpo is up to 99 cents a can. That's almost $7.00 in dog money."
— *Joe Weinstein*

42

Patterson Park

The Park

This patch of ground in East Baltimore was notorious long before 75-year old merchant William Patterson donated five acres of land to the city in 1827. In 1808 thousands of Baltimore protesters boarded the brigantine *Sophia* and carted 720 gallons of gin here to fuel a patriotic bonfire. The official public park was not a decade old when the 7th Maine Regiment camped on the grounds during the Civil War. During its golden years Patterson Park sported spectacular ornamental iron gates by the local firm of G. Krug & Son, flower gardens and fountains. City and volunteer restoration efforts are rehabilitating the 2.6-acre waterfowl pond, Tudor buildings, and well-trod grounds.

Baltimore City

Distance from the Beltway
 - 3 miles from Exit 38
Phone Number
 - None
Website
 - www.pattersonpark.com
Admission Fee
 - None
Directions
 - The park is in East Baltimore south of US 40, bounded by Park Avenue, Baltimore Street and Eastern Avenue. Parking is on the street.

The Walks

Many of the brick and asphalt paths winding through the 155-acre park are walkways based on plans drawn by brothers John Charles and Frederick Law Olmsted, Jr. n 1904. Scattered along the walkways and grassy slopes are magnificent trees dating to the original plantings when the park opened in 1853. Some of the scars and humps on the hillsides are remnants of the trenches dug during the War of 1812.

A bas-relief monument to Revolutionary War hero Count Casimir Pulaski, the "Father of the American Calvary," stands in a park corner but no tribute exists for the colorful Patterson who risked his fortune supplying Washington's troops, fought at

> **Bonus**
> Standing on the highest rise in the park where Commander John Rodgers amassed 12,000 troops to protect the city during the Battle of Baltimore in the War of 1812 is the Patterson Park Observatory. Designer Charles H. Latrobe, grandson of the designer of the U.S. Capitol, built the orange-and-yellow tower in 1891 when he was Superintendent of Parks. Latrobe embellished the tower with three tiers of balconies and enough fantail windows, lattice work and Oriental flourishes that the Observatory is more commonly known as the "Pagoda." Recently restored, visitors can climb the spiral stairs on Sundays but the view from dog's eye level outside is none to shaggy either. And you never know what you may see. In 1937 a small plane safely crash-landed in Patterson Park.

Yorktown, helped organize the B&O Railroad and endured a daughter's tragic marriage to Napoleon Bonaparte's brother.

Trail Sense: No maps and none needed.

Dog Friendliness

Scores of dogwalkers use Patterson Park and ambitious urban canine hikers can head south to nearby Inner Harbor or Fells Point.

Traffic

This is a busy urban park.

Canine Swimming

None.

Trail Time

Less than an hour.

43

Triadelphia Recreation Area

The Park

Triadelphia was once a leading Maryland mill town with a bustling population of 400. Meaning "three brothers," for the trio of brothers-in-law who married Brooke sisters and built the original mills, Triadelphia was destroyed by the same 1889 rains that ignited the famous Johnstown flood in Pennsylvania. Already in decline before the deluge, the village was not rebuilt and it was a ghost town that was drowned under the reservoir that bears its name in 1942.

Montgomery County

Distance from the Beltway
 - 25 miles from Exit 16
Phone Number
 - None
Website
 - None
Admission Fee
 - None
Directions
 - Triadelphia Reservoir is on the Montgomery County/Howard County border in the Patuxent River State Park. From Roxbury Mills Road (MD 97) cross the river and turn left on Triadelphia Lake Road to the parking lot.

The Walks

The Triadelphia Recreation Area was developed in the Patuxent Watershed for waterside picnicking and recreation. At the top of the boat launch steps lead to a linear trail that rises high above the reservoir and drops down along the Patuxent River to its terminus in a parking lot on Route 97. The route in Patuxent River State Park dips and rolls through the airy woods - few of the trees are old growth behemoths. The trail is narrow and easywalking as it skips along.

Trail Sense: No map is available but the trail is well-marked with red blazes (most helpfully placed at least seven feet high for easy spotting).

Dog Friendliness

Dogs are permitted on the trail along the Patuxent River.

> **Bonus**
> Growing unobtrusively beside the parking lot is one of the rarest native ornamental trees in the world, the Franklinia Alatamaha. A relative of the camelia, this flowering tree is prized at any time of the year - in the winter for its striped bark, in the summer for its palm-sized snow white flowers, and in the fall for its deep red leaves. The Franklinia was discovered by Philadelphia botanist John Bartram in 1765 in a remote corner of Georgia along the Alatamaha River and named for his friend Benjamin Franklin. It has not been found growing in the wild since 1790. Just to the left of these botanical marvels is the historic spring which was used as Triadelphia's water supply when the town was founded in 1809.

Traffic
Not many adventurers stop for this pleasing linear trail.

Canine Swimming
The Patuxent River provides some of the best dog paddling in the Baltimore area with easy access from grassy banks to pools and spilling water.

Trail Time
Less than an hour.

44

Ma and Pa Heritage Trail

The Park

The married couple in question are the states of Maryland and Pennsylvania which were wedded by a short-line railroad carrying freight and passengers between Baltimore and York. It took the peripatetic line 77.2 twisting miles of track to cover the 49-mile distance. The much beloved Ma and Pa operated from 1901 until 1956, hauling enough milk from area dairy farms to be known as the "Milky Way." The Foundation for the Preservation of the Ma and Pa Railroad set out in the mid-1990s to create a hiker/biker trail on seven miles of the old railroad bed in the Bel Air/Forest Hill area.

Harford County

Distance from the Beltway
- 12 miles from Exit 32
Phone Number
- (410) 638-3535
Website
- None
Admission Fee
- None
Directions
- Parking for Phase I is available at Tollgate Road opposite the Equestrian Center and on Mast Street, one block west of Route 924. To access Phase II, use Blake's Venture Park on Melrose Lane or Friends Park on Jarrettsville Road in Forest Hill.

The Walks

The Ma and Pa Trail is a stone dust path that differs from its other "rail-to-trail" brethren by its abundance of dips and swirls in the trail, a legacy of the local line's 476 curves. Much of the route is wooded although there is never a feeling of "getting away from it all" along the route. The tunnel under MD 24 was built especially for equestrians from a less congested age. There is also hiking available in 421-acre Heavenly Waters Park, although dogs are confined to a macadam trail aound the duck pond.

Trail Sense: A trail map is available for you to see where this linear trail will eventually take you. Mile markers are posted along the route.

> **Bonus**
> Standing on a hillside overlooking the Ma and Pa Trail is Liriodendron, an elegant mansion built as a summer home by Baltimore surgeon Howard Kelly to assuage the homesickness of his Prussian bride in 1897. Dr. Kelly, who pioneered the use of radium in cancer therapy and helped found Johns Hopkins Medical College, named his new escape after the tulip polar tree, Liriodendron. The couple was married for 53 years before both passed away in 1943 six hours apart, neither knowing the other was dying. A woodland trail winds around the back of the property and leads up to the grounds. It can be reached via a parking lot near the Mast Street parking lot.

Traffic
The Ma and Pa Heritage Corridor is a busy trail and you can count on many dogs, bikes, strollers and the occasional horse (in Phase 1 only).

Canine Swimming
There are no real dog dipping opportunities along the trail with only limited stream access available.

Trail Time
More than an hour.

> *"He is very imprudent, a dog is. He never makes it his business to inquire whether you are in the right or in the wrong, never bothers as to whether you are going up or down upon's life ladder, never asks whether you are rich or poor, silly or wise, sinner or saint."*
> — Jerome K. Jerome

45

North Park

The Park

On June 12, 1764 Charles Mason and Jeremiah Dixon walked into Alexander Bryan's cornfield near Newark, Delaware and planted a small concrete pillar that cemented their names in American history. The survey the English mathematicians began that day would establish the border between Maryland and Pennsylvania and forever separate the "North" from "South" in America. Today the Mason Dixon Trail connects Chadds Ford, Pennsylvania with the Appalachian Trail 190 miles away using local parks and public roads. The well-marked Mason Dixon Trail begins its jaunt up the western bank of the Susquehanna River in Havre de Grace.

Harford County

Distance from the Beltway
- 22 miles from Exit 33
Phone Number
- (410) 939-5780
Website
- www.angelfire.com/pa2/yorkhikingclub/mdts.html
Admission Fee
- Entrance fee for museum only
Directions
- North Park is in Havre de Grace on Conesteo Street, off Water Street. Follow signs for the Lockhouse Museum.

The Walks

You can pick up the blue blazes of the Mason Dixon Trail on a telephone pole in the parking lot for the Susquehanna Lockhouse Museum. Across a footbridge and past a small playground, the trail leads under the US 40 Hatem Memorial Bridge. The trail picks up an abandoned rail line used in the building of the Conowingo Dam (trees growing in the middle of the tracks should ease worries of oncoming trains). This is easy going on level ground that passes through wetlands and a mixed hardwood forest. In about one mile the trail ends for canine hikers at the base of a large rockpile - an athletic dog might make the top but the risk dwarfs the reward. The return trip can be made on a

> **Bonus**
> At this point the 444-mile Susquehanna River is busy emptying 19 million gallons of fresh water every minute into the Chesapeake Bay. It has drained that water from 13 million acres of land. The rocky river upstream from here, however, is not navigable and the 45-mile Susquehanna and Tidewater Canal was built for barges, pulled a by mules at a steady 4 miles per hour, to haul goods between Havre de Grace and Wrightsville, Pennsylvania. The first of 29 locks operated at this point and it has been restored to its original appearance including a pivoting footbridge that swung open to allow barge traffic through. The handsome brick Lock House, now a museum open on weekends, dates to the canal's opening in 1840.

wide dirt trail - probably the former towpath - on the edge of the Susquehanna River. On hot, airless summer days the stench from the flotilla of dead fish washed up on shore on this route can be overwhelming but your dog will love it.

The grounds of the museum are a good place to take the dog as well with a grassy field for a game of fetch and a small beach on the river.

Trail Sense: No maps but the trail is well-marked.

Dog Friendliness

For dogwalkers looking to experience the Susquehanna River without the crowds and formality of Susquehanna State Park this is a good place to come.

Traffic

Most walkers without dogs choose the Promenade on the other side of town.

Canine Swimming

There is plenty of good access to the Susquehanna River.

Trail Time

Less than an hour.

46
Herring Run Park

The Park

Before being annexed by Baltimore City in the early 1900s the land around Herring Run was a rural quiltwork of farms and estates. A village named Georgetown thrived in the area and near the present-day Sinclair Lane Elementary School a horse farm rented mounts for local residents to ride along the stream. Herring Run suffered considerable abuse as the city filled in around it but in recent years the park, which claims 324 acres of land along Herring Run, has regained it place of importance in the surrounding neighborhoods.

Baltimore City

Distance from the Beltway
- 5 miles from Exit 38
Phone Number
- None
Website
- www.belair-edison.org/herringrun.html
Admission Fee
- None
Directions
- The 4-mile linear park can be accessed by parking on bordering neighborhood streets on both the north and south side of Herring Run in east Baltimore. Crossroads include Harford Road (MD 147) and Belair Road (US 1).

The Walks

A paved serpentine path traces the winding course of Herring Run for 4 miles on the southern edge of the stream. Along the way are wide grassy fields and secluded alcoves of mature woodlands. To complete the entire route does involve crossing busy streets so use caution.

Herring Run Park is a magnet for dog owners in the surrounding neighborhoods and it is not unusual to happen upon a doggie play group by the waterside.

> **Bonus**
> In 1881 engineers began a reservoir system for providing Baltimoreans water by damming Tiffany's Run on the city's then norther n edge. The resulting Lake Montebello was filled by a series of brick water tunnels but only served as a reservoir for 4 years. Instead its water cleaned filter beds in the Montebello Filtration Plant. Today, in the northwest section of Herring Run Park, Lake Montebello looks much as it always has. The hike around the lake is 1 1/2 miles and there are separate lanes for walkers, runners, cyclists and vehicular traffic.

Trail Sense: There are no maps or trail markings but plenty of folks around to ask for directions in the unlikely event of a wrong turn.

Dog Friendliness
Herring Run Park is one of the best parks in the city for dogs.

Traffic
There is plenty of room to step off the trail when a cyclist or roller blader glides by.

Canine Swimming
Herring Run is ideal for doggie splashing and occasionally there are pockets deep enough for dog paddling.

Trail Time
More than an hour.

> *"No animal should ever jump up on the dining room furniture unless...he can hold his own in the conversation."*
>   - Fran Liebowitz

47
Odenton Nature Center

The Park
The undeveloped natural area at Odenton affords a leafy escape from its suburban surroundings. The park offers no amenities, including signage. Enter the woods from behind the schools or via deadends in the adjacent neighborhoods.

The Walks
This is basic backyards woods hiking with miles of ungroomed trails. Expect any surface under paw - hard-packed dirt, rocky, even sand. Any combination of loop hikes are possible on the maze of trails that scoot up and down the stream valleys.

Trail Sense: There are no maps available and no signage. Spray painted marks along the trail are hazards that have been spotted for mountain bike races.

Dog Friendliness
Dogs are welcome in this undeveloped park.

Traffic
The Odenton trails are popular with mountain bikers who sometimes stage races here.

Anne Arundel County

Distance from the Beltway
- 12 miles from Exit 4
Phone Number
- None
Website
- None
Admission Fee
- None
Directions
- This natural area is located west of Gambrills and can be accessed from the Arundel school complex off Annapolis Road (MD 175).

> **Bonus**
> Although you can turn in any direction, throw a stick and hit a housing development, you can actually descend into a feeling of wilderness in the Odenton Nature Center.

Canine Swimming
The streams at Odenton are little more than extra moist wetlands in most places.

Trail Time
More than an hour.

> *"No one appreciates the very special genius
> of your conversation as a dog does."*
> *- Christopher Morley*

48

Fort Mc Henry National Monument

The Park

Francis Scott Key was a 35-year old lawyer selected as an envoy to secure the release of American doctor William Beanes during the War of 1812. Sailing under a flag of truce, Key boarded the British flaship *Tonnant*. His mission was a success but Key was detained as the British bombardment of Fort McHenry, a star-shaped defender of Baltimore Harbor built in the late 1700s, began on the morning of September 13, 1814. After nearly two days of launching 1500 bombshells, the British abandoned their invasion. Properly inspired, amateur poet Key scribbled out the lines to the *Defence of Fort McHenry* on the back of an envelope. It became the "Star-Spangled Banner" when performed by a Baltimore actor a month later and was adopted as America's national anthem on March 3, 1931. Two years later, Fort McHenry came under the direction of the National Park Service and today is the only area designated both a national moument and historic shrine.

Baltimore City

Distance from the Beltway
 - 6 miles from Exit 3A
Phone Number
 - (410) 962-4290
Website
 - http://www.nps.gov/fomc/
Admission Fee
 - None
Directions
 - From I-95 take Exit 55 (Key Highway) to Lawrence Street. Turn left and left again on Fort Avenue to end.

The Walks

Fort McHenry rests on a 43-acre appendage of land in the mouth of Baltimore Harbor. There are large grassy open fields around the brick fort with plenty of room for romping for the dog. Cool breezes from the water and a grove of syacmore trees on the south side provide relief from the sun if needed. A concrete trail runs along all three sides of the seawall to create a loop of the park with plenty of opportunity to soak up historical monuments

> **Bonus**
> Fort McHenry sits in the heart of the Port of Baltimore where ships laden with iron ore, sugar, bananas and other commodities pay call from all over the world. Looking to the right autos unload on the Patapsco River and directly in front of you bulk container ships disgorge their cargo. Meanwhile on the water tugboats constantly orchestrate this merchant ship ballet that unfolds before you as the dog chases a tennis ball.

and shrines. A restored tidal wetland area keeps feeding and migratory birds arriving.

Trail Sense: None needed.

Dog Friendliness

Dogs are allowed everywhere at Fort McHenry except inside the fort itself but Francis Scott Key probably never set foot inside either (the National Park Service is unsure whether he did or not).

Traffic

This is a good place to socialize with other dogs, picnickers and kitefliers.

Canine Swimming

None.

Trail Time

Less than an hour.

"Dogs' lives are too short. Their only fault, really"
                                            - Agnes Sligh Turnbull

49

Druid Hill Park

The Park

The city of Baltimore paid $475,000 for the Rogers family estate in 1860 to create the jewel of its park system. Colonel Nicholas Rogers designed his property to resemble a pastoral English park and the city continued the theme with picnic pavilions, grassy promenades, statues and fountains. A massive Tuscan Doric entranceway was built of Nova Scotia sandstone in 1868 at the cost of $24,000 and Druid Lake was formed in 1871 behind the largest earthen dam in America to provide drinking water. Today the historic park covers 600 acres.

Baltimore City

Distance from the Beltway
  - 6 miles from Exit 18
Phone Number
  - (410) 396-7931
Website
  - http://baltimorecity.gov/government/recnparks
Admission Fee
  - None
Directions
  - The main entrance for the park is on Madison Avenue. Take Exit 7 west off I-83 onto Druid Park Lake Drive to entrance on right past the lake.

The Walks

There are no formal hikes in Baltimore's old dowager - just plenty of room to ramble on rolling hills. The grassy paths have been paved over and some can still be found, including a brick walkway near the tennis courts that once marked the delineation of Druid Park's "separate but equal" facilities for blacks and whites. In 1948 a crowd of 500 onlookers watched as black tennis players were carried off the "whites-only" tennis courts by police in one of America's earliest demonstrations in the civil rights movement.

The Baltimore Zoo opened in Druid Hill Park in 1876 as America's third zoo and it is possible for your dog to glimpse - and certainly smell - a few unfamiliar animals as she trots about the park. The original Federal-style Rogers Mansion House surveys

> **Bonus**
> The most unique addition to Druid Hill Park was a 90-foot tall Conservatory built of metal and glass in 1888. Known as the Palm House for its giant tropical residents, the Conservatory and attached greenhouses have been carefully restored. Even if you can't take advantage of the free admission and go inside with the dog, the glass windows surrender views of the exotic world inside.

the park from a hill near the center of the park. The walk around Druid Lake covers 1.5 miles.

Trail Sense: No maps are in the park but there are no prescribed routes to follow, either.

Dog Friendliness
Dogs are permitted in Druid Hill Park.

Traffic
Stay away from the zoo and there is plenty of room to stretch out here.

Canine Swimming
Give the dog a day off from swimming when you come to Druid Hill Park.

Trail Time
Less than an hour.

> *"Properly trained, a man can be dog's best friend."*
> *- Corey Ford*

50

Hampton National Historic Site

The Park

When Captain Charles Ridgely, heir to an iron and shipping fortune, began construction on Hampton mansion in 1783 this now highly suburbanized part of Baltimore County was so remote that wolves howled at night and locals ridiculed the project in the wilderness as "Ridgely's Folly." In 1948, after housing six generations of Ridgelys, the Georgian mansion became the first site in the National Park Service to be recognized for its architectural merit and not its historical significance. Once a sprawling, self-sufficient empire of 25,000 acres, all that remains of the original Hampton estate is 63 acres.

Baltimore County

Distance from the Beltway
- 1 mile from Exit 27
Phone Number
- (410) 823-1309
Website
- www.nps.gov/hamp/
Admission Fee
- None
Directions
- Hampton NHS is northeast of Towson. From I-695, take Exit 27-B north (Dulaney Valley Road) and make an immediate right on Hampton Lane to the entrance on right.

The Walks

The elegant stuccoed mansion is off limits to your dog but that is no reason he can't strut around the grounds like royalty. He can trot down the Great Terrace behind the house, once used for bowling on the green, and into the formal English boxwood garden. Where once a 700-tree orchard stood is an open field ideal for a game of fetch. Scattered among the 200 historic specimen trees are original outbuildings - stables that once housed Maryland's fastest horses, a citrus-growing orangery and slave quarters. On the front lawn is a grass-covered brick dome enclosing a 33-foot deep pit that was used as an ice house.

> **Bonus**
> One wonders what Charles Ridgely would think of his final resting place were he able to see it today. When placed inside the family's Greek Revival vault after his death, his land holdings included enough land to make up half of present-day Baltimore. Yet the Ridgely family cemetery now squeezes against an interstate highway with a view of a neighbor's backyard play set. Still, the brick-walled family cemetery is a unique historical destination open to your dog.

Trail Sense: A park map of the grounds points out historical sights for which there is no signage.

Dog Friendliness
Dogs are allowed to explore the historic grounds.

Traffic
Hampton is an ideal place for a solitary stroll with the dog.

Canine Swimming
None.

Trail Time
Less than an hour.

> *"If you don't think dogs can count, try putting three dog biscuits in your pocket and giving Fido two."*
>
> *- Phil Pastoret*

Before we continue on and describe 37 more place to hike with the dog, let's take a minute to list some of the parks that don't allow dogs...

No Dogs!

Anne Arundel County

Jug Bay Wetlands Sanctuary
Sandy Point State Park

Baltimore County

Hart-Miller Island State Park
(dogs are allowed on Pleasure Island, accessible only by boat and with no formal trails)
Irvine Nature Center
Marshy Point Nature Center

Harford County

Tydings Memorial Park
(no dogs on the Havre de Grace Promenade)

Patapsco State Park

Avalon Area
Hollofield Area
McKeldin Area
Orange Grove Area

37 More Places To Hike With Your Dog In The Baltimore Region

Annapolis High School Community Nature Trail
Annapolis
Anne Arundel County
Riva Road off Allen Boulevard (MD 665)

Located behind the school is a country trail leading to the edge of Broad Creek. Comprised of dirt, grass and mulch the trail winds in and out of the woods for 1.5 miles. Part of the South River watershed, this gift to the community from the students features wooden bridges over the small streams and wide trails.

Arden Park
Crownsville
Anne Arundel County
Sunrise Beach Road off Generals Highway (MD 178)

Walk through the small playground at the back of the park and begin hiking on hard-packed dirt trails in the Severn Run Natural Environment Area. The paths follow a ridge high above the Gumbottom Branch valley. There are plenty of ups and downs on these wooded trails, among the most remote in the Baltimore area. The routes are unmarked and eventually dead-end against horse farms or roads.

Broadneck Park
Cape Saint Claire
Anne Arundel County
College Parkway

A rolling asphalt trail circles this 57-acre recreational park. Most of the hiking is open among the ballfields but one quieter section slips into some woods in the western end of Broadneck. There is no water available on this easy-walking route. To the left as you enter the park is Anne Arundel County's second dog park with two enclosed off-leash play areas - one for large dogs and the other for small and elderly dogs.

Carroll Park
Baltimore
Baltimore County
Monroe Street and Washington Boulevard

There are no paths at all in Carroll Park, a recreation park that brashly calls itself the "Pride of Parks." Dog owners ignore the bustling recreational games below and make their way to the forgotten back of the park, on the hillside where Mount Clare stands. Built in 1754 by Charles Carroll, the Georgian mansion is the only remaining colonial building in Baltimore. Once 360 feet long, only the center of the mansion still survives. Dogs can romp in the grassy expanses and ornamental stone ruins where oranges, lemons and even pineapples once grew. Where a visiting George Washington (the ivy on the outside walls came from his home at Mt. Vernon) once stood looking over the Patapsco River you can stand surreally in the only 18th century plantation existing in a major American city and look down on 21st century PSI Net Stadium.

Catonsville Community Park
Catonsville
Baltimore County
Rolling Road off Frederick Road (MD 144)

Frederick Road, just south of the Catonsville Community Park, was once the main road west from Baltimore and travellers fancied a tasty cornbread served up by a local inn so much the town was originally known as "Johnnycake." Located behind the Catonsville Senior Center, the park offers a Community Nature Trail that runs into and through a stream valley. The old park could stand a little sprucing up, especially in the wetlands, but your dog won't notice. The trails cover about a mile in the woodlands.

Cedar Lane Park
Columbia
Howard County
Cedar Lane Road off Clarksville Pike (MD 108)

Cedar Lane, on the edge of the planned city of Columbia, features 100 acres about evenly divided between playing fields and mature woodlands. Little light filters through the canopy of the tall hardwoods to the paved asphalt trails. The paths curve and roll but come to an end all too quickly. There is no water along the trails.

Chesterwood Park
Dundalk
Baltimore County
Chesterwood Road off Peninsula Expressway (MD 157)

This pretty little picnic park belies its industrial surroundings. Although void of trails, this is one of the best "fetch" parks around with an expansive grassy area and excellent access to the calm waters of Bullneck Creek. In fact, if county officials somehow lost their minds and turned the entire park, which already shares space with the county park maintenance department, completely over to dogs, it would be one of the best dog parks anywhere. As it is, someone else may have already considered the thought - the "DOGS MUST BE LEASHED" line on the Rules and Regulations board was painted out during our visit.

Christmas Tree Park
Manchester
Carroll County
Victory Street and York Street off Main Street (MD 30)

You can't hang lights and tinsel from these 60-foot firs but the sweet scent will linger as you work your way past the picnic pavilion to unmarked trails in the woods. In the adjoining forest is a small pond that launches Grave Run on its journey to Prettyboy Reservoir. There is plenty of space to roam in the developed areas of this recreational park but still less than an hour of hiking time.

County Home Park
Timonium
Baltimore County
Van Buren Street and Alms House Road of York Road (MD 45)

This park looks promising from the parking lot behind the Baltimore County Historical Society, converted from the last almshouse in the county. Spread before you are paved paths running in concentric circles up a groomed hillside, two duck ponds, a shaded picnic area. But once the trails reach the top of the hill they run out quickly against the Longview Golf Club. The dog can sit and watch putting action on the par-3 5th green and drives up the hill from the tee on the 6th hole but there is little else to do here.

Crofton Park
Crofton
Anne Arundel County
Davidsonville Road (MD 424), north of Defense Highway (MD 450)

Designed after World War II in the manor of an English croft (a small piece of pasture), the bustling community has long since outgrown its pastoral ideal. Canine hikers can still get a feel for the English highlands at Crofton Park, where the paved walking path is distinguished by others of its ilk by tall trees. The trail also leads over wetlands and around a reflecting pond in a clearing in the woods.

Deer Creek Park
Dublin
Harford County
Sandy Hook Road off US 1

Beyond a garbage can in the small parking area, there are no amenities in this park. Deer Creek completes two horseshoe bends at this point in its journey to the Susquehanna River and the undeveloped park sits inside the two shoes. A scruffy trail leads along the water to one of the best doggie swimming pools in the region (beneath a rope swing) and continues to a rocky conclusion around the bend. Several trails radiate off this level path to the left, all leading steeply to a point on top of a wooded knob overlooking Deer Creek. There is nearly an hour of secluded hiking here.

Edgewater Village Park
Edgewood
Harford County
Brookside Drive and Tree Top Road off Pulaski Highway (US 40)

A paved path circles a man-made pond for more than a mile in this 55-acre residential park. On sunny days the light glistening off the water is matched sparkle for sparkle by the broken glass on the trail. Shopping carts and assorted junk washed ashore do nothing to enhance the dog walking experience here, either. A community clean-up would go a long way towards making this a pleasant stroll with the dog.

Font Hill Wetlands Park
Ellicott City
Howard County
Font Hill Drive off Frederick Road

Tucked in the middle of a suburban neighborhood, Font Hill Wetlands Park offers a unique 20-minute canine hiking diversion. A series of grass and asphalt and wooden boardwalk paths wander around two open ponds and richly vegetated wetlands. This tiny oasis in suburbia is apparently easier to spot from the air than the road because Font Hill supports a diverse visiting bird population. Parking is on the neighborhood streets.

Forest Hill Recreation Complex
Bel Air
Harford County
Rock Spring Church Road off Rock Spring Road (MD 24)

A 50-acre playground essentially given over to ballfields, the adventurous canine hiker can find a reason to visit Forest Hill, especially on uncrowded weekday mornings when the park will be yours. Behind the playing fields, downhill from the parking lot, lies a rudimentary trail working along the wooded slopes. The trail is ungroomed and you will snap many sticks and crunch plenty of leaves underfoot. Although blazed with yellow stars, red circles, green boxes and blue triangles it is a single trail. When ready to return to your car, you will find yourself having covered about two miles of hiking.

Fort Armistead Park
Baltimore
Baltimore County
Fort Armistead Road off Hawkins Point Road

Fort Armistead, named for Major George Armistead who commanded Fort McHenry during its bombardment in the War of 1812, was constructed during the Spanish-American War. Stripped of its cannon in 1903, the army left the fort in 1921. The four abandoned batteries in the fort-turned-park have since been put to use as canvasses for graffiti artists. For dogs the highlight is a small, scruffy beach with access to the Patapsco River. While the dog is in the waves, you can study the Francis Scott Key Bridge above you and Fort Carroll in the middle of the Patapsco. The artificial island was built under the direction of United States Colonel Robert E. Lee between 1849 and 1852 but the fort was never completed.

Fort Smallwood Park
Rockwood Beach
Anne Arundel County
end of Fort Smallwood Road (MD 173)

As part of the necklace of forts around Baltimore, the United States Army acquired 100 acres here at the mouth of Rock Creek in the 1890s. Named in honor of Major General William Smallwood of the Continental Army and governor of Maryland in 1785, the base remained active until 1926 when it was sold to the city for use as a park. The fortifications remain to be hiked around but beach activities are the main attraction of the park. Fort Smallwood Park is considered to be the best spot on the East Coast to observe migrating raptors in the spring.

Generals Highway Corridor Park
Crownsville
Anne Arundel County
Crownsville Road between Generals Highway (MD 178)
and Defense Highway (MD 450)

Generals Highway picked up its name from Revolutionary times when the Colonial road was used by French General Rochambeau to reach the climactic siege of Yorktown in 1781 and two years later when American Generals Horatio Gates and William Smallwood led George Washington along this route to resign his commission before the Continental Congress in Annapolis. Today the park is a busy recreational center with a paved loop circling the property. The circuit is highlighted by the weathered 19th century graveyard of the Duvall family, including Samuel C. Duvall, aged 22, who died in the second day of fighting at Gettysburg on July 2, 1863.

GORC Park
Gambrills
Anne Arundel County
Strawberry Lake Way off Waugh Chapel Road

This modern recreation park features Rend Way, an exercise path around the 47.7 acre property. The paved path is an open hike for all but a few steps of the way, although there is a pleasing grove of maple trees between the baseball fields. There is no water along the path as it visits each corner of the Gambrills Odenton Recreation Council Park.

Gorman Area Park
Dickinson
Howard County
end of Kindler Road off Johns Hopkins Road

This undeveloped area on the south bank of the Middle Patuxent River features several miles of shaded hiking out and back along the water. The trails are old fisherman's paths on narrow dirt that roll moderately along. When you reach down to the shoreline the dog paddling is excellent. This is mostly easy going on lightly used trails.

Gunpowder Falls State Park - Dundee Creek
Chase
Baltimore County
end of Graces Quarters Road off Eastern Avenue (MD 150)

Dogs are not allowed in the adjoining Hammerman Day Use Area of the state park. But go past the Hammerman entrance and make the second right to the Dundee Fishing Area and there is an attractive nature trail that welcomes dogs. Mostly an old access road, the trail is wide and soft on the paw as it circles through mixed pines and hardwoods. Blazed in white, there is about a half hour of hiking on the trail, which offers access to small beaches on the quiet Dundee Creek.

Gwynn Oak Park
Woodlawn
Baltimore County
Gwynn Oak Avenue (MD 126)

Mostly a picnic park, a short paved trail runs along Gwynns Falls, which is dammed in the park to form a small impoundment pond. Across the bridge is a rogue trail to the left that beckons the adventurous canine hiker; take it only as far as the dam. After that the trail narrows until it disappears completely in the wetlands.

Gwynnbrook Wildlife Management Area
Owings Mills
Baltimore County
Gwynnbrook Avenue at Owings Mills Boulevard

In 1919 the state of Maryland purchased 290 acres of land here to propagate rabbits and bobwhite quail as game. It was the first land set aside for wildlife management in Maryland. The centerpiece of today's 70-acre Gwynnbrook Wildlife Management Area is a backyard nature tour called the Wild Acres Trail. Dogs are not welcome on this trail but canine hikers can use a semi-maintained old access road past a fishing pond and up a hill through yellow poplar and red maple. There is nothing special about this short hike, save its conclusion at the base of a massive transmission tower belonging to Maryland Public Television.

Hanlon Park
Baltimore
Baltimore County
Longwood Road off Hilton Road

The highpoint - literally - of 100-acre Hanlon Park is the Forest Park reservoir, familiarly known as Lake Ashburton. Unlike more celebrated paths, such as the one around Lake Montebello across town, the broken asphalt path affords constant views of the sparkling clear water behind an iron fence. Below Lake Ashburton the park drops away dramatically and the canine hiking becomes less structured amid crumbling walls and paths. The reservoir dates to 1911.

Hugg-Thomas Wildlife Management Area
Sykesville
Howard County
Forsythe Avenue off Sykesville Road

The Hugg-Thomas Wildlife Management Area covers 276 acres in two separate parcels bordering the Patapsco River. Unmarked trails, mostly old grass farm roads, circle the rolling woodlands. Near the western border of the park a side trail leads to a hilltop through which the Baltimore & Ohio railroad has tunnelled for only a few hundred yards making it a simple matter to watch a passing train go through both sides. Songbirds find the forest especially appealing and flock to Hugg-Thomas, as do those who watch them. Also frequenting the miles of trails are hunters after deer, rabbits and turkeys. Due to hunting restrictions the trails are frequently closed from September to February and in early spring.

Leight Park
Abingdon
Harford County
Otter Point Road off Pulaski Highway (US 40)

One of the last remaining expanses of freshwater tidal marsh in the upper Chesapeake Bay, Leight Park features 672 acres, 62 of which are wooded uplands overlooking Otter Point Creek. For nearly a century the land was in the Leight family, who lived here trapping and farming and fishing. In 1981 the property was donated to Harford County which created the Anita C. Leight Estuary Center to facilitate research on the Bay. Dogs are welcome on the nicely groomed nature trail, with wood chips laid beneath lumbering river birch and black willow and, further from shore, mountain laurel and Virginia pine. The Center, however, is only open to the public on Saturdays from 10:00 a.m. to 5:00 p.m and 12:00 noon to 5:00 p.m. on Sunday.

Mariner Point Park
Joppatowne
Harford County
Kearney Drive off Joppa Farm Road

You are ushered into this 38-acre peninsular park by a wooden 7-foot tall seaman, resplendent in a sturdy yellow slicker. The prime attraction within is a 2 1/2-mile hiking trail that slithers through the property. The path gets plenty of wear from dog walkers, joggers, strollers and other recreational travelers. Paved for most of its journey, the trail becomes an attractive boardwalk as the the land surrounded by Taylors Creek, Foster Branch and the Gunpowder Falls juts into the water. These waters made Joppatowne a major port in the early 1700s but when the Gunpowder Falls silted up, most of the commercial traffic drifted south to Baltimore. There is no access to the marsh or open water but the quiet views are splendid.

Miami Beach Park
Bengies-Chase
Baltimore County
Miami Beach Road from Bowleys Quarters Road

Dogs are not permitted on the beach or swimming areas of this neighborhood park on the Chesapeake Bay. But the 59-acre grounds feature an open grassy area and trails through light woods that welcome dogs. The trails unfortunately resemble a garden planted with rusting appliances and rotting carpet remnants. The park is open daily from 10 a.m. to 7 p.m. only and the entrance is gated, although if you absolutely have to get in a quick hike earlier you can access the woods.

Parker Conservation Area
Norrisville
Harford County
Jolly Acres Road, west of Norrisville Road (MD 23)

This hilly parcel of land is conserved as a 159-acre undeveloped park by Harford County. There are no parking lots and spaces along the road are few; a good spot to stop is near the bridge over Deer Creek, which flows energetically through the property. A short trail leads upstream on the north side of the bridge past ruins and impressive rock outcroppings before concluding in a marshy area. An overgrown access road leads from the ruins up the wooded hillsides to more trails. Nothing is marked and there is an hour or more of exploring here.

> *"A dog teaches a boy fidelity, perserverance, and to turn around three times before lying down."*
>
> *- Robert Benchley*

Patuxent Ponds Park
Woodwardville
Anne Arundel County
Patuxent Road off Conway Road (MD 424)

This small 9.8-acre park offers a grassy trail around two woodlands ponds. The Patuxent Ponds are home to an active colony of beavers and their toothwork is much in evidence out in the water and along the banks. It is not unusual to observe the popular rodents, North America's biggest, swimming in the open water as well. In times of high water it is possible to complete 95% of the circumnavigation of the ponds and be cut off from returning to your car but the short hike is appealing enough that retracing your steps will be a welcome imposition.

Provinces Park
Jessup
Anne Arundel County
Disney Road off Annapolis Road (MD 175)

A multi-use trail circles this recreation park for a mile, partially in the open and partially in the shade. Some of the wooded fringes serve up a pine scent from a coniferous woodland and a small wetland also enhances the hike. The full trip can be circumvented by a short cut trail midway through the circuit.

Robert Copenhaver Park
Joppa
Harford County
Trimble Road off Magnolia Road (MD 152)

A narrow 24-acre park framing the Foster Branch stream valley as it makes its short journey to the Gunpowder River, Robert Copenhaver Park is strictly for residential dog walkers. A macadam creekside trail slips through a canyon of backyards and there are some rogue trails behind the ballfields. A small duck pond suitable for doggie dips nudges this small park out of the ranks of neighborhood parks.

Rockfield Park
Bel Air
Harford County
Churchville Road (MD 22)

Rockfield is a recreational park with a playground and ball diamonds but does feature a short, secluded macadam trail along a stream valley. Rogue natural trails of grass and dirt lead to a hilltop with a commanding view of the surrounding countryside, including the namesake Rockfeld Manor, a 1921 prairie-style home. More undeveloped trails dip into a mature woods at the back of the 46-acre park with a small stream for canine splashing. You can do worse when on the prowl for a quick dog hike in Harford County.

Rocky Point Park
Essex
Baltimore County
Rocky Point Road off Back River Neck Road

Although its 375 acres on the shores of the Back River and the Chesapeake Bay hold great promise, there isn't a lot here for the active dog owner. Much of the scenic park is given over to a golf course and there are no maintained trails. Dogs are permitted in the picnic areas but there isn't much room to race around. Dogs are not permitted in the sandy beach area and there is limited access to the surrounding water elsewhere. But if you are looking for a quiet picnic spot on the water with the dog, this is the place. A daily fee is charged from Memorial Day to Labor Day.

Scott's Cove
Scaggsville
Howard County
Harding Road off Old Columbia Pike and Columbia Pike (US 29)

The Washington Suburban Sanitary Commission allows recreational activities at the T. Howard Duckett (Rocky Gorge) Reservoir, including hiking. Scott's Cove, on the Howard County side of the reservoir, is devoted mostly to picnicking with a small smattering of dirt trails through the wooded shoreline. When the water level drops, it is possible to hike along the pebbly shore (watch for paw-piercing glass) around the reservoir. On the Montgomery/Prince Georges side are a system of bridle trails as well.

Silver Creek Park
Pikesville
Baltimore County
end of Silver Creek Road off Milford Mill Road

Sudbrook Park was designed in 1899 by Frederick Law Olmsted as one of the first planned suburban communities in the United States. The neighborhood features curving roads that cascade against the parkland. With Silver Creek Road closed off the suburban park is traffic-free. There are large grassy areas amidst mature trees for games of fetch and access to Gwynns Falls for canine dog-paddling. The short trail connecting Silver Creek and Sudbrook parks is part of the Gwynns Falls Greenway.

"The best thing about a man is his dog."
- French Proverb

Stansbury Park
Dundalk
Baltimore County
Stansbury Road off Chesterwood Road exit from
Peninsula Expressway (MD 157)

This park stands out from the run-of-the-mill recreational park by way of a pleasing pond circumnavigation that connects it with adjoining Lynch Cove Park. Strip away the driving range and the power lines and place this reedy waterside walk in a gated Florida community and it would be a major selling point. There are even some moderate rises in elevation for panoramic views and good access from the stone and dirt path to the water for a doggie dip. Colorful local legend holds that the pond, once known as Emala Lake, was a former quarry that flooded almost instantaneously, trapping workers beneath 200 feet of murderous water. Alas, the pond formed more mundanely when sand was excavated to build the nearby Peninsula Expressway in the 1950s and a spring was struck at the bottom of the hole. The water filled at a decidedly less lethal pace and after several months reached its current depth of about 20 feet. Stansbury Park also offers large grassy fields suitable for canine romping.

Swan Harbor Farm
Havre de Grace
Harford County
Oakington Road off Pulaski Highway (US 40)

Currently maintained by the county as a gentleman's farm, most of Swan Harbor Farm's 463 acres are undeveloped. Walking trails surrounding the growing fields are planned; until their creation you can take a short path used by generations of family farmers to small stone beaches on the Chesapeake Bay for some of the best dog-paddling in Harford County.

Sykesville Town Linear Park
Sykesville
Carroll County
Harlan Lane off Kalorama Road

The area that would become Sykesville was jump-started by the arrival of the Baltimore & Ohio Railroad which built its first line along the Patapsco River in 1830. Most of the original town was destroyed by flooding in 1868 and it was rebuilt on the river's north shore. Much of Sykesville today, including the only surviving Queen Anne-style brick B&O Railroad Station designed by E. Francis Baldwin, is an historic area. Unfortunately this 1.5-mile macadam path runs straight through a residential area and doesn't touch the historic area. The trail is slightly rolling and shaded.

Thomas Point Park
Highland Beach
Anne Arundel County
Thomas Point Road off Arundel on the Bay Road

In 1665 merchant Phillip Thomas was granted 120 acres of land between the Severn and South rivers known as Fullers Poynt. Over the decades the land at the mouth of the South River took on the Thomas family name and three centuries later 44 acres of the original land grant became Thomas Point Park. A nature trail winds .3 of a mile down the wooded peninsula to its grassy conclusion. Visible from the point in Chesapeake Bay is the Thomas Thomas Point Lighthouse, first commissioned in 1875. One of only two cottage-style screwpile lighthouses on its original foundations on the Chesapeake, the iron pilings of the white hexagonal building are screwed directly into the bottom of the bay. It was the last lighthouse on the Bay to be automated and was saved from demolition by public protest in 1972. Return trip can be made along a natural surface access road.

Twin Oaks Park
Severna Park
Anne Arundel County
Peninsula Farm Road off College Parkway

You can cobble together a mile of quiet (when the middle school across the street isn't letting out) walking on a mosaic of macadam trails here. The trails wind through a mix of woods and grassy areas; the "twin oaks" are along the road just before the entrance but the park also boasts an impressive collection of pines and gums as well. Hiking at Twin Oaks is flat and easy and includes a big sand area in the playground for doggie digging.

Dogs At The Atlantic Ocean

Delaware Beaches

Bethany Beach — No dogs on the beach or boardwalk from April 1 to October 1

Dewey Beach — Dogs are not allowed on the beach between 9:30 a.m. to 5:30 p.m. in season

Fenwick Island — No dogs permitted on the beach from May 1 to September 30

Lewes/Cape Henlopen — From May 1 to September 30 no dogs are allowed on the beach between 8:00 a.m. and 6:30 p.m.

Rehoboth Beach — Dogs are prohibited from the beach and boardwalk from April 1 to October 31

Maryland Beaches

Assateague Island National Seashore — Dogs allowed on beach but not on the trails

Assateague State Park — No dogs allowed in park

Ocean City — Dogs allowed on beach and boardwalk from October 1 to April 30

Tips For Taking Your Dog To The Beach

- The majority of dogs can swim and love it, but dogs entering the water for the first time should be tested; never throw your dog into the water. Start in shallow water and call your dog's name - or try to coax him in with a treat or toy. Always keep your dog within reach.

- Another way to introduce your dog to the water is with a dog that already swims and is friendly with your dog. Let your dog follow his friend.

- If your dog begins to doggie paddle with his front legs only, lift his hind legs and help him float. He should quickly catch on and will keep his back end up.

- Swimming is a great form of exercise, but don't let your dog overdo it. He will be using new muscles and may tire quickly. If your dog is out of shape, don't encourage him to run on the sand. Running on the beach is strenuous exercise and a dog that is out of shape can easily pull a tendon or ligament.

- Be careful of strong tides that are hazardous for even the best swimmers.

- Cool ocean water is tempting to your dog. Do not allow him to drink too much sea water. Salt in the water will make him sick. Salt and other minerals found in the ocean can damage your dog's coat so regular bathing is essential. Bring fresh drinking water to the beach.

- Check with a lifeguard for daily water conditions - dogs are easy targets for jellyfish and sea lice.

- Dogs can get sunburned, especially short-haired dogs and ones with pink skin and white hair. Limit your dog's exposure when the sun is strong and apply sunblock to his ears and nose 30 minutes before going outside.

Dog Parks

Dog parks often begin as informal gatherings of dog owners that eventaully become legitimized by local government. Anne Arundel County leads the way in dog park creation in the Baltimore area but citizen activists in many places in the region are advocating for future dog parks. These parks currently allow dogs off leash in designated dog parks:

Quiet Waters Park (see page 82)
- two large fenced enclosures, one for large dogs and one for smaller and elderly dogs
- small sand beach available nearby for swimming
- no lights; closed at dusk
- admission fee to park; closed Tuesdays

Broadneck Park (see page 136)
- fenced enclosures
- dirt and grass surface
- no lights; closed at dusk
- no fee; open 7 days a week

Downs Memorial Park (see page 36)
- no fenced enclosures
- sand beach open for dogs on Chesapeake Bay
- admission fee to park; closed Tuesdays

Tips For Enjoying Your Visit To The Dog Park

- Keep an eye on your dog and a leash in hand. Situations can change quickly in a dog park.

- Keep puppies younger than 4 months at home until they have all necessary innoculations to allow them to play safely with other dogs. Make certain that your older dog is current on shots and has a valid license.

- ALWAYS clean up after your dog. Failure to pick up your dog's poop is the quickest way to spoil a dog park for everyone.

- If your dog begins to play too rough, don't take time to sort out blame - leash the dog and leave immediately.

- Leave your female dog at home if she is in heat.

- Don't volunteer to bring all the dogs in the neighborhood with you when you go. Don't bring any more dogs than you can supervise comfortably.

- Observe and follow all posted regulations at the dog park.

Index To Parks

Anne Arundel County — page

Annapolis High School Community Nature Trail	136
Arden Park	136
Baltimore & Annapolis Trail	108
BWI Trail	100
Broadneck Trail	136
Crofton Park	139
Downs Memorial Park	36
Fort Smallwood Park	142
Generals Highway Corridor Park	142
GORC Park	143
Kinder Farm Park	104
Lake Waterford Park	88
Patuxent Research Refuge (North Tract)	58
Odenton Nature Center	124
Patuxent Ponds Park	148
Provinces Park	148
Quiet Waters Park	82
Thomas Point Park	152
Truxtun Park	68
Twin Oaks Park	151

Baltimore City — page

Carroll Park	137
Cylburn Arboretum	62
Druid Hill Park	128
Fort Armistead Park	141
Fort McHenry National Monument	126
Gwynns Falls Park	94
Hanlon Park	145
Herring Run Park	122
Leakin Park	94
Patterson Park	114

Baltimore County — page

Benjamin Banneker Historical Park	86
Catonsville Community Park	137
Chesterwood Park	138
County Home Park	139
Cromwell Valley Park	54
Double Rock Park	78
Fort Howard Park	92
Gunpowder Falls State Park (Belair Road)	42
Gunpowder Falls State Park (Dundee Creek)	144
Gunpowder Falls State Park (Hereford)	32
Gunpowder Falls State Park (Jerusalem Mill)	64
Gunpowder Falls State Park (Pleasantville)	76
Gunpowder Falls State Park (Sweet Air)	38
Gwynn Oak Park	144
Gwynnwood Wildlife Management Area	144
Hampton National Historic Site	130
Liberty Reservoir	96
Loch Raven Reservoir	52
Miami Beach Park	147
North Point State Park	98
Northern Central RR Trail	90

Index To Parks

Baltimore County

	page
Oregon Ridge Park	40
Prettyboy Reservoir	80
Robert E. Lee Park	30
Rocky Point Park	149
Silver Creek Park	150
Soldiers Delight NEA	50
Stansbury Park	151

Carroll County

	page
Christmas Tree Park	138
Gillis Falls Reservoir Site	106
Hashawha Trails	60
Morgan Run NEA	70
Pine Valley Nature Center	102
Piney Run Park	56
Sykesville Town Linear Park	152

Harford County

	page
Deer Creek Park	140
Eden Mill Nature Center	76
Edgewater Village Park	140
Forest Hill Recreation Complex	141
Leight Park	146
Ma and Pa Heritage Trail	120
Mariner Point Park	146
North Park	120
Parker Conservation Area	147
Robert Copenhaver Park	148
Rockfield Park	149
Rocks State Park	66
Susquehanna State Park	34
Swan Harbor Park	151

Howard County

	page
Cedar Lane Park	138
Centennial Park	110
Font Hill Wetlands Park	140
Gorman Area Park	143
Hugg-Thomas Wildlife Management Area	145
Middle Patuxent Environmental Area	72
Patapsco Valley State Park	44
Rockburn Branch Park	84
Savage Park	48
Schooley Mill Park	112
Scott's Cove	150
Triadelphia Recreation Area	116

About The A BARK IN THE PARK Series

Cruden Bay Books publishes guidebooks for canine hikers in communities around North America. For more information on A BARK IN THE PARK books please visit our website at **www.hikewithyourdog.com**. At the site you can find:

- direct links to more than 2000 dog-friendly parks
- dog regulations for national parks in the United States and Canada
- recommendations for favorite hikes and can share your favorite hike with your dog with others
- beach regulations for dogs on more than 1500 Atlantic Ocean, Pacific Ocean, Gulf of Mexico and Great Lakes beaches
- tip sheets for going on a hike with your dog

Cruden Bay Books
PO Box 467
Montchanin, DE 19710
Phone: 302-999-8843
Fax: 302-326-0400
E-mail: crubay@earthlink.net
www.hikewithyourdog.com

Want to order A BARK IN THE PARK books for your organization? Quantity discounts available.